D1241506

LET ME TELL YOU ABOUT MY SAVIOR

YESTERDAY, TODAY, AND FOREVER

WHEN THE KING WAS CARPENTER

LET ME TELL YOU ABOUT MY SAVIOR

YESTERDAY, TODAY, AND FOREVER

WHEN THE KING WAS CARPENTER

MARIA VON TRAPP

New Leaf Press

First printing: September 2000

Copyright © 2000 by New Leaf Press. All rights reserved. No part of this book may be used or reproduced in any manner whatsoever without written permission of the publisher except in the case of brief quotations in articles and reviews. For information write: New Leaf Press, Inc., P.O. Box 726, Green Forest, AR 72638.

ISBN: 0-89221-501-1
Library of Congress Number: 00-106228

Yesterday, Today, and Forever: copyright © 1975.
When the King Was Carpenter: copyright © 1976.

Unless otherwise noted, all Scripture references are from the Revised Standard Version of the Bible.

Printed in the United States of America.

Please visit our website for other great titles:
www.newleafpress.net

For information regarding publicity for author interviews contact Dianna Fletcher at (870) 438-5288.

PUBLISHER'S PREFACE

There is something magical about childhood memories; the grand ones seem to get better with time and the not-so-grand seem to fade away. As a parent I believe one of the most important things that you need to do with your children is build memories.

I was very blessed to have two wonderful, loving parents who provided me with some great memories as a child. I traveled the Far East with my father when I was only 12 or 13, going to Japan, Korea, Taiwan, and Indonesia. We went on some great fishing trips to Canada and many other intriguing places, but one of my fondest memories is our trip to Stowe, Vermont, and the Trapp Family Lodge.

The year was 1975. I was 14 years old and on my way from Harrison, Arkansas, to Stowe with my father, Cliff Dudley. He had just started his own publishing company and we were traveling to the home of one of our very first authors. The company was New Leaf Press and the new author was Maria von Trapp. I was really excited because *The Sound of Music* was the very first movie I had ever seen at a movie theater and now I was going to meet the real-life Maria. This would begin a two-week period of firsts: meeting Maria, my first taste of wine, my first mass, my first time to snow ski, and my first game of Scrabble.

Everything was blanketed in soft, billowy snow as we traveled through Vermont. (I can remember Maria saying later that week, "There is always snow in Stowe.") As we turned a corner, the quaint, rustic lodge came into view. The architectural style of it made us feel as though we had left Vermont and were now entering Maria's hometown of Salzburg, in Austria.

We settled into the lodge that afternoon, and then looked around the majestic grounds. Everything was simply beautiful. We were still gazing at the panoramic view in this idyllic setting when we were called for dinner. I can still remember the warmth from the many fireplaces, the aroma of dinner, and my own nervousness as I prepared to meet Maria. *What will she be like? What do I say? I hope I don't do anything to embarrass myself.*

Maria entered the room with a warm smile and my nervousness was quickly forgotten as she heartily greeted us. I first noticed her Austrian attire (which looked odd to me, but it was her everyday clothing), but her pleasantness and sincerity pervaded my thoughts and I began to feel comfortable in my new surroundings. Her features were striking and there was a beauty about her that is not easily described because it is that inward beauty from the heart that radiates through a person's whole being.

As we ate, she and my father talked of many things, and soon the conversation included me as she told me of the things pertaining to skiing which I could do during my stay. My instructor ended up being a young woman in her thirties who actually *had* skied on the Austrian Olympic team. Wow!

As the two weeks unfolded, I skied every day all day long, first cross-country and then downhill. I can remember the building where all of the skis were stored and the smell of the wax that they put on the skis for the cross-country skiing. It was a wonderful time for a 14-year-old boy.

While I worked on my skiing, Maria and Dad worked on *Yesterday, Today and Forever.* The eighth book published by New Leaf Press, it accounted for the early success of the company, selling over 200,000 copies the first year. That was over 25 years ago, and we are still going strong. Thanks, Maria!

In honor of the memories of Maria and the 25th anniversary of New Leaf Press, we are releasing a gift edition of the first two books that we did with her 25 years ago, *Yesterday, Today and Forever* and *When the King Was Carpenter.* Maria passed away in 1987, and my father passed away five years later in 1992, but I know both of them would be very pleased with the work of this company which they helped start a quarter of a century ago.

Tim Dudley
President

Yesterday, Today
and Forever

Contents

HOW IT HAPPENED

I t was in Italian South Tyrol in a primitive little country inn on the edge of a lovely village in the mountains. The year was 1938, and this was the first station on our flight from Nazi-invaded Austria. We, that is Father Wasner, my husband, and I, and nine children with the tenth on the way, had just barely arrived at this peaceful little place when it happened. With a terrific wail, Lorli, aged six, discovered that we had forgotten her favorite toy, a worn-out, shapeless, hairless something, formerly a teddy bear.

The grief of a child is always terrible. It is bottomless, without hope. A child has no past and no future. It just lives in the present moment — wholeheartedly. If the present moment spells disaster, the child suffers it with his whole heart, his whole soul, his whole strength, and his whole little being. Because a child is so helpless in his grief, we should never take it lightly, but drop all we are doing at the moment and come to his aid.

I remember the situation so well, the glassed-in veranda in which we were standing, and me looking for a cookie or a candy, and there was none. Had I forgotten that we were refugees now, and luxuries like candies were things of the past? But even if the hands of a mother are empty, her mind and heart must never be. Taking the sobbing little girl on my lap, I said: "Come, Lorli, Mother is going to tell you a story."

That had always worked; but now it only brought forth new tears, and violently shaking her little head with its mop of dark curls, she shrieked, "I don't want to hear about Cinderella or Snow White — I want. . . ."

"Oh no, Lorli," I said, "I'm not going to tell you one of those stories; but if you will listen to me, I will tell you the story of another child like you to whom the same thing happened — oh, a wonderful story!" And as I said this, I had no idea of what I was going to tell.

"Once upon a time," I began, "there was a mother, a father, and a little child."

"A girl?" Lorli managed to ask between sobs.

"No, a boy," I said.

At this very moment I saw them right before me, the Holy Family on their way to Egypt. For the first time, however, I didn't think of them the way the holy cards pictured them — Mary in blue, Joseph in brown, the little child in pink, each one with a golden hem on his garment — riding complacently on a neat donkey through a beautiful countryside full of date palms. For the first time it dawned on me that they were really refugees like millions of people nowadays, like ourselves, for instance.

"Flee," said the angel to Joseph, "flee into Egypt, for Herod will seek the child to destroy Him."

Wasn't the fright which must have chilled Joseph's blood at the moment, the same fright which we had experienced so often when we heard the cruel stories of how the Gestapo was on somebody's heels, how they had dragged away fathers or brothers from families we knew? Wasn't it the same fright which had finally gotten us across the border? The angel had not announced to Joseph just exactly what Herod intended to do, but Joseph knew that Herod's Gestapo worked fast, and that his reputation for cruelty was unequaled. If the parents wanted to save the child, they had to hurry to get away from Herod; and while I told my little girl the story of the flight into Egypt, I listened to it myself. It was so new, so not at all holy-card-wise. It was so excitingly modern, the story of refugees, who, after having reached the goal, Egypt, became displaced persons — D.P.s. It was a story full of anxiety and homesickness, but also full of trust in the Heavenly Father, who in His own good time, provides a home for all refugees.

Lorli had long since stopped crying. In rapt attention she listened to my description of the dangers of the flight. I told about the wild animals and robbers, the terrific heat at noon and the cold at night on that dangerous passage through the desert, which even the Roman soldiers dreaded, and how the little boy did not make any fuss over a missing a toy, not once.

Then the angel of the Lord appeared again to Joseph, in my story, and bade him to return home.

"Will an angel tell our father, too, when we can go back to Salzburg?" asked Lorli eagerly.

"Yes," I said without the slightest hesitation, and a happy little girl glided down from my lap and ran off to Stefan, the innkeeper's little boy, to tell him this, her newest story.

Some of the older children had moved over from the other side of the veranda during the story.

"Mother, that was really exciting," they said. I was completely taken with it myself. During the telling it had become clearer in my own mind: This story isn't over yet. All this is still going on.

"Children," I said, "I feel as though we were at the beginning of a great discovery. It seems as if Herod isn't really dead. He keeps living under different names, like Saul and Nero, or Hitler and Stalin. He still seeks the child to destroy Him." How close Our Lord and His family had become all of a sudden when we met them as fellow refugees!

That was a big discovery, and it came to us on the very threshold of a new life when we had joined the millions of refugees on the highways and byways of Europe in search of a new home. But I have told about all this in another book, *The Story of the Trapp Family Singers*, and I don't want to repeat any of it here. This is to be simply the story of how "Jesus Christ is the same yesterday and today and forever" (Heb. 13:8) — finally became a member of our family.

In that summer of our flight through Europe we had another startling experience. It was a few weeks after the incident on the glassed-in veranda. One of our sons was engaged to be married, and his bride-to-be spent several weeks with us in Holland. One day she came to me and said, "Mother, can you tell me what he was like when he was a baby? He has told me everything about his life as far as he can remember, but — I want to know all."

That hit me right between the eyes. Reading the Gospels together and searching in them for more modern stories like the one of the flight into Egypt had become a family hobby by then. Merely by doing it we had found out how little we knew about our Lord and His family, His country, and His times. Aside from stating the fact, we hadn't done anything about it. Then came this girl who went out of her way to find out every detail about the one whom she loved because — "she had to know all." This did something to us.

"How can we pretend to love our Lord," we said to

ourselves, "if we don't want to know all about Him as well?"

On that same evening during night prayer it occurred to me that Mary, the mother of Christ, was a mother like me. Perhaps she would be just as pleased about the questioning as I had been, and so I turned to God and said, "Father, there is so little written in the Gospels about your Son when He was a Child and while He was growing up. How was it in Nazareth, in Bethlehem, in Egypt? Was He lively or was He rather quiet? What did He eat, what did He wear? What did He do all day long, and what about Joseph?

I don't believe in chances and coincidences. It must have been she who gave two friends of ours, independently of each other, the idea to present us with books: *The life of Our Lord Jesus Christ* by the German Jesuit Maurice Meschler, and *Life of Jesus* by Francois Mauriac.[1] There could hardly be found a greater contrast than between those two works on the same subject. That was the beginning of a very helpful little library of our own. After we had finished these two books, we wanted to know more. And more. And more. God has never stopped answering our questions. Besides helping us to find the right books, He also helped us to remember what we had once learned in history, geography, archaeology, and religion. He drew our attention to the fact that besides the four canonical Gospels there is something else which we can almost regard as a "fifth Gospel," so much a source of information it is: the Holy Land itself. Very much of it is still exactly the same as it was in His time. There we started getting interested in maps of the modern and ancient Holy Land.

Many years have passed since. After we had shared with Him the anxiety of the flight, we lived through years of the "hidden life," and then through the excitement of the "public life." Many notebooks have been filled with information which we drew out of different books, which seem to complement each other. Pictures of the Holy Land have been cut out of magazines throughout the years, and postcards sent to us from there by friends have been collected. Putting all these different pieces together is like assembling a crèche.

Every time we say the Creed, we say towards the end that we believe in the communion of saints.

Of the Early Church it is said, "The multitude of them that believed were of one heart and of one soul: neither said any of them that ought of the things which he possessed was his own; but they had all things common" (Acts 4:32). That did not refer only to money and the things money can buy, but also and foremost to spiritual goods. We know from the Acts and Epistles of the Apostles and the writings of the early fathers that this was true. Haven't we moved far away from those times? While we still might share our earthly possessions and contribute to collections, we certainly are not in the habit of sharing our spiritual goods any more. This is our innermost private life, and what I learned this morning in meditation or what occurred to me during reading is nobody's business. This is the spirit of "I-me-myself," whereas the right spirit is always "we-our," as we find in the liturgy, in the prayers of the Church. This would make the difference between a family and a group of people living together under one roof.

It is in this spirit that we want to share with you our great discovery — the bringing of the Holy Scriptures to life for us, and, by watching Him, learning to imitate Him, learning how to live, how to love, how to die. In the world situation of today it may look like five minutes to twelve, but if we Christians would wake up to the meaning of our name and become "other Christs," we might bring about what was promised only to men of good will: peace on earth.

PART ONE

YESTERDAY

"In Those Days"

Whenever we read the life story of one of the great ones, be it Washington, Lincoln, Napoleon, or Julius Caesar, we always find that the biographer takes pains to picture for us the time in which his hero lived, thus helping us to understand certain features of his character and certain happenings of his age. So Luke, the biographer of Christ's childhood, does the same. "In those days," he says, "a decree went out from Caesar Augustus that all the world should be enrolled" (Luke 2:1).

"In those days." That means the time when in Rome the nephew of the great Julius Caesar had become emperor. His real name had been Octavius, but his soldiers hailed him as "Augustus." In those days the Roman troops had been victorious almost to the ends of the then-known world. They had invaded country after country in many bloody wars, but now the whole empire was at peace. Before Augustus came into power, terrible civil wars had raged.

These and all the invasions had exhausted the finances of the empire, and so Caesar Augustus used this new peace to think of new means to fill the coffers of the state. His new idea was to get every single one of his subjects, without exception to make a contribution. To help the publicans, or tax collectors, in their business, he ordered now, like the owner of a big department store, an inventory to be made.

"In those days a decree went out from Caesar Augustus that all the world should be enrolled" (Luke 2:1).

"All the world" — what a proud phrase! But these were almost the facts. Almost all of what was then known of the world was ruled by Roman governors according to Roman law, and the Roman legions watched on the borders.

In those days one of the most important provinces was Syria, and the official in charge of the census in this province was Quirinius. Tucked away in one corner of his province was a tiny little kingdom of Judea, with Herod as its king.

When Caesar Augustus decided on the census, messengers on horseback galloped along the famous Roman highways carrying the new law north and south. At the same time, fast galleys left the Roman ports to take the message across the seas. One of them would arrive in Syria, and Quirinius would sub-delegate King Herod to carry out the census in his land. Herod, who owed his kingship to the Romans, would be only too eager to oblige.

These enrollments were usually made in the places where the people lived. But the Jews had a different custom, and it had always been the policy of the Romans to respect the local habits and customs of conquered nations. Since ancient times the Jews had been divided into tribes. To each tribe belonged a certain county of Judea/Samaria with a family headquarters.

Joseph belonged to the tribe of Judah and to the house

and family of David. The place where David the king had been born and raised was Bethlehem, which later became the headquarters of the House of David. When, therefore, on a certain winter day a messenger came to Nazareth, the little town of Galilee, reading aloud to all the men the imperial decree, "all went to be enrolled, each to his own city. And Joseph also went up from Galilee, from the city of Nazareth, to Judea, to the city of David, which is called Bethlehem, because he was of the house and lineage of David, to be enrolled with Mary, his betrothed, who was with child" (Luke 2:3–5).

CHAPTER 2

THE HOLY LAND IN WINTER

When my husband was still in the navy, he once spent some time in the Holy Land. It proved to be wonderful for us later.

When, for instance, we wanted to find out about that winter journey of Mary and Joseph from Nazareth to Bethlehem, we simply said, "Tell us, what is the Holy Land like in winter?"

"Oh well," he used to say, "that depends upon where you are. Small as it is, the country has three distinct zones. There is that deep gully, the Jordan Valley, below the level of the Mediterranean. There it is always covered with snow. The weather there I found very much like the Alps. At the same time there is the rather mild climate in the hill country, Galilee, Samaria, and Judea. But why do I say 'mild'?" he corrected himself. "In the winter, that means in the rainy season, it can be simply awful. The rains start in October and last until March. 'It never rains but it pours,' one can really say of those tropical showers. The winds blowing down from the mountains are ice-cold."

"It was about 30 years ago," said my husband meditatively, "when our ship anchored in the Bay of Haifa, and all the officers were invited by some Arab sheik to make a trip on horseback throughout the country. That was before the times of modernization. No bulldozers had yet reached the Holy Land and we were assured time and again that what we saw was pretty much as it had been since time immemorial.

"We were there around Christmastime. The rainy season had been going on for almost three months, and the moment one left the highway, the horse sank in the deep mud. We were astonished to find everywhere the peasants in their fields plowing and sowing, and we asked why they didn't wait for the dry season. But we were told that the sun bakes the earth so terribly that the primitive plows couldn't break the hard soil. I remember we usually saw groups of plowmen working together with their tiny oxen and little plows, merely scratching furrows. We used to stop our horses and watch them for a little while. Often they were shivering in the cold. One old man I remember was holding a basket of seeds, and with tears in his eyes, complained to our interpreter about the weather. When I think of him now in his brown woolen tunic, soaked through and heavy with rain, I can imagine what Joseph must have looked like."

From there we went on to figure it all out for ourselves: Mary and Joseph locking up their little house in Nazareth and setting out in the rain on their 80-mile trip. Mary was in no condition to travel. She expected her child any day now, but obviously the census was meant for men and women alike, and Mary, knowing that the Messiah had to be born in Bethlehem, knew she had to go. They were not rich enough to afford camels, the only convenient way of travel in those days, but they took a donkey. No saddles or stirrups were used at that time. Mary had to sit on a folded blanket laid across the sharp-pointed back of the little animal. How long would it have taken them to reach Bethlehem? From the writings of Julius Caesar we know that the Roman soldiers were supposed to make 20 miles daily when they were not armed, and 12 miles a day under arms. But those were sturdy, strong young men, and here was a young mother expecting her first child within a few days. She surely couldn't make more than 12 miles a day.

When we, the entire family, traveled all over South America it also happened to be in the winter, in the rainy season. If one was caught in a tropical shower, one was drenched within a few minutes. A few short hours after Mary and Joseph had left the houses of Nazareth behind them, the rain must have soaked their woolen mantles and woolen tunics, and the hooves of the little ass spattered mud on them. The garments would never become quite dry until they had reached Bethlehem. Heavier and heavier they would hang on their shoulders, as the mud crust became thicker every day.

Such a trip was not without its dangers in those days. Only since the Crusades, in the 12th century, have lions become extinct in the Holy Land. Throughout Holy Scriptures we find warnings against lions, wolves, and other wild animals. Maybe Mary and Joseph did not always reach an inn, and they had to camp out one or more nights on the roadside. Then a fire had to be made and kept going throughout the night to keep the wild animals away.

There was another pest of the highway — the robbers. The country was infested with them. Large bands of them lived in the hills and threatened the travelers. When we say "inn," we must not think of a comfortable, homey, New England cottage-like building. We mustn't even think of a building at all. The inn by the roadside in the Holy Land consisted usually of a wall 12 to 15 feet high, surrounding a quadrangle, in the middle of which a big fire was burning. The innkeeper let the travelers in who, for a small payment, would spend the night around the fire, unmolested by robbers and wild animals. But they had to provide their own food, and the only comfort was freedom from fear.

Mary and Joseph wound their way slowly down the hills of Galilee through the plains of Estralon towards the hills of Judea. It must have been very hard for Mary to sit for hours at a time with no rest for her back, being bounced by the hard, mincing steps of the little donkey. She might lean on Joseph's shoulder for a little while; he might help her down so she could walk a bit. But wading through the mud didn't help much either, so she would go back to the donkey, always patient, with a weary little smile. But it must have torn Joseph's heart to see her uncomfortable like this, and be unable to do much to help. His whole heart must have been longing for Bethlehem, his hometown, where his father's house was still standing and his brothers and kindred were still living. If only they were safe in Bethlehem, then everything would be all right. The family would provide fresh, dry clothing, and in the privacy of her own room, Mary would quickly recover from the hardships of this trip.

These might have been the thoughts of Joseph as he was leading the donkey by the reins up and down the hills through the rain and wind for eight, nine, or maybe ten long days, while Mary's heart repeated over again and again, "Behold, I am the handmaid of the Lord; let it be to me according to your word" (Luke 1:38).

"Pray that your flight may not be in winter" (Matt. 24:20), our Lord would admonish His listeners later. It seems that His mother must have told Him about her unforgettable trip from Nazareth to Bethlehem — in winter.

CHAPTER 3

AWAY IN A MANGER

Is it true what Rupert said," asked young Martina woefully, "that in the Holy Land around Christmas it is always warm like in summer, and roses and violets bloom in Bethlehem? On all Christmas cards Bethlehem is deeply covered with snow, and in our Christmas carols it's always a white Christmas, and I like that much better."

"No, it's quite possible that the first Christmas was a white Christmas, too," answered Father Wasner. "In the book of the Maccabees it is written, 'But there fell a great snow and he' — Tryphon — 'came not into the country of Galaad' " (1 Mac. 13:22). Father Wasner, who had fled Austria with our family and was the conductor and composer for the Trapp Family choir, often added insight to our conversations.

"And Flavius Josephus, who was a citizen of Jerusalem one generation after our Lord, says that in Jericho down at the Jordan there is always a wonderful temperature, that the people there are only dressed in linen, 'even when snow covers the rest of Judea,' " said I, who had gotten a popular edition of the works of Flavius Josephus for Christmas.

Agathe added, " Only recently I read in a book that an officer wrote home that when he came out from midnight mass in Bethlehem, he saw snow covering the ground."

Snow or no snow — it doesn't seem so very important, but it certainly was a help to us in picturing Mary and Joseph traveling through the short, cold December days towards Bethlehem. Everybody likes to see his hometown again. Once, when we went back to our hometown, Salzburg, in Austria, everyone in the family afterwards confessed the same thing: how his heart was beating faster as the train drew closer; how eagerly he was looking out for the first landmark, the fortress; how he was hoping to find the countryside the way we had left it years ago. And we had an American friend with us, Hester, to whom we now proudly pointed out the sights.

Once outside of Jerusalem, there were only six more miles to go, and Joseph must have glanced eagerly southward to see whether he could see the first familiar landmark, the pillar over Rachel's sepulchre.

"Salzburg is a very old place," we explained with pride to Hester, "fifteen hundred years old."

The same thing Joseph could have said to his bride from the north, because Bethlehem was an old place already when, a thousand years before them, their ancestor David watched the sheep in the fields outside the little town. After five miles the road turns sharply to the east, and there they saw a brand new building towering over David's town. It was the Herodeum, a combination of fortress and mausoleum, recently erected by Kind Herod, who was dying inch by inch on his couch of gold.

And now they had reached the end of the journey. The

little town of Bethlehem lay before them, terraced on the slope surrounded by vineyards and olive groves. They entered through the city gate. How many, many times during the last days Joseph must have gazed anxiously at his young wife, who each time had smiled bravely back at him. But now all was safe, and his heart was full of thanksgiving. One could imagine that they first wound their way through the crowded streets to the publican's office to fulfill the census which had brought them thither, and then Joseph must have said, "And now, let's go home."

To the Oriental, hospitality is sacred. If there was no room for Joseph in the house of his fathers, it must really have been occupied to the last square yard by relatives who had arrived for the same purpose a little earlier. If one has been in Salzburg during Festival time, or in Oberammergau when the Passion Play is on, and has seen on almost every house sign "No Room — No Room — No Room," then one can imagine a little bit how it must have been. Joseph, pleading from door to door, worming his way through the crowds with his broad shoulders making a way for Mary, who shouldn't be pushed like that. Only after he had tried all the houses of relatives and friends, Joseph decided with a deep sigh to go to the public inn.

Bethlehem, unlike Jerusalem, was only a small country place and didn't have one of those larger and more comfortably equipped tourist homes. There wouldn't be any privacy for Mary. There wouldn't even be cleanliness with all the fresh and rotten manure around the walled-in courtyard. But there was only the choice between the protecting walls of this little inn or the dangers of the open fields, and one more look at Mary showed that she was drooping with fatigue. And then the most crushing of all blows came. There was no room at the inn. Maybe the innkeeper, whose place was overcrowded, didn't even open the door, but through the closed door told them harshly to go away. If the onslaught of tourists becomes too great in a small town, the natives often object. If you haven't wired ahead for reservations, well, that's just too bad.

"He came to his own home, and his own people received him not" (John 1:11).

Joseph had been chosen by God Almighty to be the guardian of those two most precious lives — the Son of God and His mother. This was now the hour when Joseph showed that he was worthy of his high vocation. In this moment of his keenest disappointment it would have been only human and most understandable if he had lost his nerve a bit and tried once more from house to house, making a big display, imploring, threatening, crying (we are in the Orient!). No, Joseph did not leave Mary's side. Boys growing up in country towns usually know every square foot of the surroundings for miles. He must have known those limestone caves in which his great ancestor David had hidden, and he remembered the one where there was a manger. Once more Joseph took the reins of the donkey and silently led the way towards the only shelter he could provide.

Once when we had come to that point in the Christmas story, Hedwig, who was pretty young then, exclaimed with flashing eyes, "Oh, Mother, if only we had lived in Bethlehem then! We would have taken Mary and Joseph into the big guest room with the balcony." Her little sisters had tears in their eyes, tears of wrath against the bad people, tears of pity for the poor mother.

Many big and little children must have felt the same way, because there is an age-old folk custom called the "*Herberg suchen*" (seeking for shelter). During the last ten days before Christmas throughout the villages of Austria the people carry an image of Mary through the place. It is left in another house each day, where it is received with great solemnity, being treated as a special guest, given a place of honor, and lovingly decorated with flowers and candles. It is also done in large families, every member taking turns for one day being the special host of the exalted guest.

Our Lord himself foresaw this reaction of the human heart when He one day would say, "And whoso shall receive one such little child in my name receiveth me" (Matt. 18:5;KJV). He does not say: "Whosoever receiveth one of those little ones in my name is doing something very nice and I will bless him for it." He says, "receiveth me." Just why don't we take Him literally? If we did, for instance, there couldn't possibly be any little ones left in the expanses of New York City throughout the hot summer months, playing on the streets in the blue fumes of the exhaust pipes, on the asphalt softened by the heat. The stone-hard asphalt can soften — how about human hearts?

Aren't Mary and Joseph still going from place to place looking for shelter, and isn't it still true that there is no room in the inn? The only change is that this time the innkeepers are we . . . you and I.

The Trapp children, left to right: Martina, Johanna, Hedwig, Werner, Maria, Agathe, and Rupert.

CHAPTER
4

SILENT NIGHT, HOLY NIGHT

I come from Tyrol. This is the part of Austria with the highest mountains and the greatest number of woodcarvers. Woodcarving seems to be a talent that is inheritable. There are whole valleys where all the families carve. The favorite objects are the very end and the very beginning of redemption — the crucifix and the crib. Tyrol is the country of the Christmas crib. Every home and every church has such a representation of the Nativity, more or less elaborate, more or less artistic. But always the cave is freshly painted and meticulously clean, ox and ass look well-groomed, and the straw may even be a little gilded. When one grows up among those "pretty" cribs, one easily forgets how different it must have been on that first Holy Night. Because there was a manger in the cave, it must have been used for animals, so the floor was littered with dung. Except for that manger, there was nothing in it perhaps but a little barley straw. The only fresh air came through the narrow entrance by which one stepped down into that dark, smelly hole. "To make oneself at home" was quite impossible. Joseph could only try to make Mary a little less uncomfortable by arranging the straw so that she could lean against the wall opposite the entrance, get some fresh air, and look up into the cold winter sky.

The Gospels don't mention the ox and ass, without which every crib would be unthinkable, but Isaiah the prophet knew of them: "The ox knoweth his owner, and the ass his master's crib" (Isa. 1:3;KJV). The Gospels also do not mention the cave directly, still, tradition very often supplements the Gospels. After all, didn't John the Apostle say that the world itself could not hold the books that would have to be written if everything should be told in detail? And it is according to tradition of the very first centuries. Justinius the martyr, living in the generation after the Apostles, and after him Jerome, living in a cave outside Bethlehem himself for most of his life, reverently describes this cave of the Holy Night.

What may have gone on during these next hours of the most holy of all nights? "And so it was," says Luke (2:6-7), "that, while they were there, the days were accomplished that she should be delivered. And she brought forth her first-born son, and wrapped him up in swaddling clothes, and laid him in a manger." And tradition adds that Joseph, who saw that the hour was at hand now for the young mother and who did not know that she wouldn't need any aid, went over to Bethlehem to look for a helper among the women. Mary, however, was drawn in deepest recollection into God, and when she came out of ecstasy, before her lay her little child. With indescribable happiness she must have taken Him to her heart, and wrapped Him up against the cold. When Joseph returned, he found mother and child. Forgotten now was the anxiety of the last days, the crushing disappointment of the evening, the coldness of the hearts in Bethlehem, as well as the cold of the frosty winter night. In this cave there was only love and wonder and adoration. For "the Word became flesh and dwelt among us . . . we have beheld his glory" (John 1:14).

CHAPTER 5

ANGELS WE HAVE HEARD ON HIGH

Christ was born in Bethlehem, but the world didn't notice. The world was asleep. "The light shineth in darkness; and the darkness comprehended it not" (John 1:5;KJV).

Only a few miles away in Jerusalem the house of the Lord God was silent and dark. The priests of the Most High were asleep. Also, the king's palace was dark. Herod was seeking relief from his pain in sleep. All the great ones in Israel, the scribes, the doctors of the law, the zealots, the Pharisees, and the Herodians — all were fast asleep. In the little town on the hillside where the family of David the king was gathered together, everybody was fast asleep. All those of the house and family of David had come, some of them from faraway places, to be enrolled as subjects of a foreigner. Now they slept, and didn't know that their kinsman promised from of old was born in their midst in a cave because there was no room in their homes, in their hearts.

In faraway Rome, Caesar Augustus was also fast asleep. Little did he know how much his recent law had inconvenienced a humble couple somewhere near the border of the empire. And little would he have cared, had he known. Wouldn't he have been astonished, though, had he learned that throughout the centuries millions and millions would come and go who would never have heard of him, the great Augustus, except in connection with the birth of this humble child!

All the great ones of this world were asleep, but in heaven was such rejoicing as never been heard since the creation of the world. All those millions of souls, perhaps headed by Adam and Eve, thanked God in a thunderous chorus that their redemption was at hand. And the Heavenly Father wanted to congratulate His children on earth — was there no one awake to receive His messengers?

"I thank thee, O Father, Lord of heaven and earth," Our Lord would pray on a later day, "because thou hast hid these things from the wise and prudent, and hast revealed them unto babes" (Matt. 11:25;KJV). And Paul would add one day: "God hath chosen the foolish things of the world to confound the wise; and God hath chosen the weak things of the world to confound the things which are mighty; And base things of the world, and things which are despised, hath God chosen"(1 Cor. 1:27–28). The great teachers of the day, the rabbis of Israel, had declared the shepherds as "base" and "foolish," the very lowest of the low, on the same level as the Gentiles, unclean before the law. And these shepherds were the only ones awake in Israel. "And there were in the same country shepherds abiding in the field, keeping watch over their flock by night" (Luke 2:8;KJV).

This was no ordinary flock they were watching. These sheep were not to be eaten by men, but they were destined to become sacrifices for God. At this time the priests of

Jahweh were not only servants of God, but also extremely successful businessmen. They had managed to become the sole proprietors of the herds from which the sacrifices were chosen. Again, it is Josephus Flavius who mentions that at one Passover around 120,000 lambs were slaughtered. That gives a little idea of the size of the flocks, parts of which were grazing on the fields outside Bethlehem. "Behold the Lamb of God," John the Baptist would exclaim later. And there the Lamb of God was born next to the lambs of sacrifice, the fulfillment next to the symbol. But it was the shepherds, not the owners, who would find out about Him first. "And, lo, the angel of the Lord came upon them, and the glory of the Lord shone round about them" (Luke 2:9;KJV).

This was not the first time that angels had been sent to men. Throughout the pages of the Old Testament we find it happening many times, but each single time when heaven and earth met, the reaction of earth was the same: "And they feared with a great fear."

"We shall surely die, because we have seen God," cried the father of Samson (Judg. 13:22;KJV) because an angel had appeared to him and his wife. How did he know that it was not God himself? And each time heaven would say to earth: "Fear not, for behold, I bring you good tidings of great joy." Each time except once. Once the great angel of the Lord was sent on a special mission into a small village tucked away in the hills, to a young girl, and this time when the natural and supernatural world met, it was different. The girl did not fall on her face, fearing she must surely die, and the first words of the angel were not "Fear not." Only once did it happen that the angel of the Lord greeted one of the children of men, and this young girl did not say to the tremendous heavenly guest in the usual bashful way, "Oh no, no sir, not you should greet me, but I have to greet you first." No, she listened to the greeting, and then she only pondered in her heart what it might mean. For in this one case the angel of the Lord was greeting Mary of Nazareth.

But the shepherds were afraid with the fear of Samson's parents. How must that have been when the brightness of God shone round about them? It is quite good to stop for a moment at such expressions and let our imagination take over. What have we seen in our life which we would call bright? The noonday sun on a summer's day on top of a glacier? The explosion of an atomic bomb? Compared with the "brightness of God," they must be like the flicker of a little candle. And this is what the shepherds saw. And what did the angel himself look like? The shepherds don't tell, but Isaiah, hundreds of years before them, had once had a look at the seraphim and described them: "Each had six wings: with two he covered his face, and with two he covered his feet, and with two he flew" (Isa. 6:2).

And who was this angel? We don't know for sure, but tradition has it that it was Gabriel, the angel of the incarnation. Now the angel talks; and again let us use our imagination and think of different voices we have heard and which we still remember for their beauty of tone. And again we may be sure that this angelic voice ringing out loud and reassuringly through the night must have been more beautiful that anything we can remember. "Fear not," the angel said, "for, behold, I bring you good tidings of great joy, which shall be to all people. For unto you is born this day in the city of David a Saviour, which is Christ the Lord" (Luke 2:10–11;KJV). It is true that these shepherds were illiterate, and for this they were cursed by the scribes. But this message they did understand, because they had been waiting all their lives for this Christ the Lord, that He might come and redeem them from the unbearable burdens which the Pharisees themselves would not deign to carry.

"And this shall be a sign unto you," continued the angel. "Ye shall find the babe wrapped in swaddling clothes, lying in a manger" (Luke 2:12;KJV). Now the shepherds knew they would not have to go into town and knock from door to door. If He was lying in a manger, it could only be in a certain cave not far away. So the Messiah had come — not as a king on horseback, and not like Melchisedec appearing in great dignity suddenly and mysteriously, but as a little baby wrapped in swaddling clothes, exactly as one of their own children was wrapped up and carried around by their wives.

The very moment when the great angel had finished his message there burst suddenly forth a torrent of heavenly music, and when the shepherds looked up in still more wonder and awe, they saw what the evangelist would describe as a "multitude of the heavenly host" (Luke 2:13;KJV). Daniel of old, when he had once had a similar vision, tried to describe it: "A stream of fire issued and came forth from before him; a thousand thousands served him, and ten thousand times ten thousand stood before him" (Dan. 7:10). That must be about a "multitude of the heavenly host." And they were now "praising God and saying, 'Glory to God in the highest, and on earth peace among men'" (Luke 2:13–14). What a choir! And this was the only time the heavenly multitudes are known to have chanted for the children of men. When Isaiah heard them, he said: "And they cried one to another and said : Holy, holy, holy is the Lord of hosts; the whole earth is full of his glory. And the foundations of the thresholds shook at the voice of him who called" (Isa. 6:3–4). Again, we might stop for a moment and think of the choirs we have heard in our life: small choirs, large choirs, men's, women's, children's voices — chanting in unison, or singing in parts. And as all human brightness was dimmed when compared with the brightness of God, so all created melody faded before the chant of heaven. There we remember the story told about young Mozart when he came to Rome and listened for the first time to the Sistine Choir performing the *Miserere,* composed by Allegri exclusively for the Sistine Chapel. Under threat of excommunication it was forbidden to copy this great work. Mozart, after having listened to it once, returned to his hotel room and wrote it down from memory. What a pity that none of the shepherds handed on the song of the first Gloria!

And what happened then? When the angels left the shepherds, there was no argument, no round-table discussion with which we people of later centuries so often kill the sound of the heavenly message in our hearts. They simply "said to one another, 'Let us go over to Bethlehem and see this thing that has happened, which the Lord has made known to us.' And they went with haste, and found Mary and Joseph, and the babe lying in a manger. And when they saw it they made known the saying which had been told them concerning this child" (Luke 2:15–17).

We don't have to say, "Oh, I wish I had been there." It is not over yet. Christ the Lord is still being born to us, if we just learn to see Him lying helpless and in poverty. Then it could be said of us also what we can say of those shepherds: "Blessed are the eyes which see what you see! For I tell you that many prophets and kings desired to see what you see, and did not see it, and to hear what you hear, and did not hear it" (Luke 10:23–24).

CHAPTER
6

MARY PONDERED IN HER HEART

There is a certain flavor to the days after a child is born into a home. Gratefulness that all went well, a deep relief from anxiety, a new happiness, and a more tender love hover over the household. All this must have been true of the very first Christian family who ever lived, only much more so. Of the young girl mother it is told that she didn't need any help, neither for herself nor for her little child. She was able to take care of Him alone right away. "And she gave birth to her first-born son and wrapped him up in swaddling clothes, and laid him in a manger" (Luke 2:7).

We can imagine Joseph going into Bethlehem every day, partly to buy fresh food, and partly to watch how the census was going. In 40 days he would have to present mother and child in the temple, and from what they had just gone through on their winter's journey, they decided to wait in Bethlehem. Of course, Joseph was trying to get his family out of the cave, and so he kept looking for a house.

45

At the same time he may have been looking for a job. When he came back from his trips into town, he told Mary that the shepherds couldn't get over the things they had heard and seen in that unforgettable night, and had told their friends and neighbors. "And all who heard it wondered at what the shepherds told them" (Luke 2:18). What did Mary do about this? She "kept all these things, pondering them in her heart" (Luke 2:19).

The way people react to important happenings in their lives, may they be exceedingly happy or sad, gives the deepest insight into their character. Let's just look around us. What is the usual reaction among our friends and neighbors if in a family something unexpected happens? Let us say the father of the family suddenly loses his whole fortune, or he is unexpectedly promoted to a big job. What is the usual reaction? Telephone and telegraph are immediately put to work, letters are written by the score, and the incident is discussed for days on end. It is no wonder that there is no time left in which to ponder on what it might mean, what message God might want to bring home to us by permitting this or that to happen in our lives.

"To ponder" is just another word for "to meditate on" or simply "to think about." With a special effort, some of us might set aside 15 minutes a day out of a sense of duty to ponder upon divine things. This time of mediation can turn into a real bother, and we may spend it looking at the watch. At the slightest provocation we gladly omit it. We are very easily "too busy to keep it up." But with Mary it seems to be second nature. Already, as a child in the temple, she must have been meditating on the law of the Lord all the days of her life, as it says in Psalm 118. The splendor of the house of God, the starry sky at night, the countryside of Judea, the Word of God as it was read to her from ancient scrolls by her teachers — everything was one big meditation book for her, telling of the grandeur and also of the mercy of God. She never grew tired of pondering on all those things in her heart.

If we would only give it a try and introduce this attitude into our homes, families, and schools again, and teach our children to think things over in their hearts! The Quakers do it — why not all of us? This is an all-but-forgotten art in our days. Who thinks? We don't need to any more. The TV and radio do it for us, and the daily papers, magazines, digests, and quite recently, digests of digests. Once when we attended a symphony concert at the Academy of Music in Philadelphia, a lady tapped me on the shoulder and said, "Baroness, I would be very much obliged if you could tell me what I should think about this concert." It sounds funny, but one should not laugh, one should cry at such poverty. How different it was with Mary, who started a life of pondering early in her youth!

There must have been visitors in the cave in that first week, only simple people because the highbrows didn't have anything to do with such castaways as the shepherds. Visiting in the Orient is identical with bringing gifts, and the shepherds give milk, butter, cheese, and bread, as the carols tell us.

While Mary and Joseph were tending to the simple chores of those days, cleaning out the cave, tending to the child, tending to the animals, receiving the shepherds with their families and friends, the king of Israel in his palace, thousands of God's priests, and all those scribes and Pharisees only a few miles away, didn't know what the smallest shepherd child in the valley of Bethlehem knew. This is the secret of God, who can only be found and recognized by simple hearts.

Toward the end of this week Joseph had to make preparations for the circumcision. This was a ceremony of the pious Jews which goes back to Abram. He was once called out of his tent at night and God told him, " 'Look toward heaven, and number the stars, if you are able to number them.' Then He said to him, 'So shall your descendants be' " (Gen. 15:5). There the first covenant, "The Old Testament," was contracted between God and men. At this time Abram was given a new name, Abraham. This is the origin of the custom that a Jewish child is given his name at his circumcision.

On the evening before that day, it was customary throughout the country for the parents of the baby to invite the children of the neighborhood for a party. The new baby was shown to them. So Joseph went out to invite the children of the shepherds, and when they came, Mary and Joseph entertained their little guests and showed them their newborn baby. And they still do so year after year, Christmas week having become a big children's party all over the world.

The circumcision was performed by the Jewish priests or elders in the homes of the people, not in the temple or synagogue. We know from Luke that when little John was circumcised, there was a great feast with all the friends and neighbors present. Such family feasts are always accompanied in the Orient by a meal, and there is always a crowd of poor people gathered at such events, sure of some alms.

On the eighth day Joseph went to Bethlehem and returned with a priest and a woman who assisted at such occasions. They brought the circumcision stool and a slab of stone around two feet in diameter, the circumcision stone, and there was a knife and a few boxes with ointments. A small carpet was spread on the rough floor of the cave, and everything was set up. The priest took the child out of the arms of the mother. They prayed and sang for some time, and then the priest asked the father which name the child should be given. "Jesus," said Joseph, as it had been announced by the angel. The woman showed the troubled young mother how to attend the wound, then they wrapped the child tightly in red and white swaddling clothes, and the ceremony was over. With the gifts of the shepherds, they arranged now a little meal, and the rest they gave to the poor. The child was crying and restless, and Mary and Joseph tried to soothe Him by carrying Him up and down the cave.

Suffering had entered into this little family. Suffering calls forth compassion; compassion, however, deepens love. This is the way it works in every ordinary family, and this is exactly the way it happened in the Holy Family. Oh, we can't start soon enough to get these three persons out of the picture frames, down from the niches, and let them become again what they really were — breathing, warm-blooded people with hearts full of emotions. There was in the cave on that day a father, a mother, and a little child. What might they have said and done to each other, and what might they have said and done to the little baby? I can't forget how one of my children once said, "In the Holy Family they never laughed or cried, did they?"

"They most certainly did," I answered with emphasis. "Why not?"

"But weren't they too holy?" Asked the little one with awe.

It is all so wrong; and the statues in the churches, and the pictures in the books have a great deal to do with it. But let us get down to facts. When God in His eternal wisdom resolved to redeem mankind, He had infinite ways in which to do it. There were shapes and forms we can think of, such as sending the Messiah as an angel in great power and glory, or as a mighty king on horseback, then there are many more possibilities which we in our limited mind can't even conceive. But no, Almighty God chose none of those ways, but instead, sent His only Son as a little child into a family.

Men have founded orders, congregations, and organizations; God's own foundation is the Christian family. A real mother, a real father, and a real child, living, loving, suffering — not symbols, but people like us. If this was God's own and only choice from those myriad, infinite possibilities, then we should say, "Amen, so be it."

"For God so loved the world that he gave his only Son, that whoever believes in him should not perish, but have eternal life" (John 3:16). Only then does it make sense that God became man and cried as a little baby in His mother's arms. If we do this, we shall very soon find how we keep pondering in our hearts, because there will be so very much to ponder about that one short life won't be time enough. It will take eternity.

CHAPTER
7

THE PURIFICATION AND
THE PRESENTATION

There are many things we really don't know about the childhood story of our Lord and there is absolutely no way of finding out. For instance, how long the census may have taken in Bethlehem, how long the little town was overcrowded, and how soon Joseph could take his family from the cave into a house. In a way it doesn't matter, and in a way it does. As soon as you have started to re-live the life of our Lord together with your family as closely as possible day by day — you discover that this is something, which has a beginning but no end. The more one has found out, the more one still has to find out. As soon as the children's interest is aroused, questions will never cease. This is a typical one: How long was the Holy Family in the cave? Once in a while it will happen that even after much research you will have to say, "I really don't know"; but this is already great progress compared with those who, when asked this same question, answer, "What do I care?"

Our children wanted to have a day by day account. Now the priest of the circumcision has left with the woman and the implements. What happened next? We figured out together that the next days and nights might have been pretty unquiet with a sick baby in the house. When the wound had healed the little Jesus smiled again; how relieved Mary and Joseph must have felt.

"And how about the census?" asked one of the youngsters. "Didn't Joseph have to go downtown and announce the new name?"

This was a good question. Surely Joseph had to do that, and so we accompanied him "downtown" to Bethlehem, as he approached once more the census taker, and watched how for the first time in history the holy name was written down. This was not an uncommon name, and in the way of His days it was spelled Joshua or Jeshua.

Even if we don't know how long it was — we may be sure it was as soon as possible — until Joseph got his little family into a house in Bethlehem. The next thing was to find out how the house in Bethlehem looked. With the help of pictures from illustrated articles and postcards sent by friends from their pilgrimages of the Holy Land, we easily found out what the houses looked like.

What I am telling here does not refer to the happenings of one year. It also is not storytelling to children. It is honest-to-goodness research work done by a whole family throughout the years. Your interest, once aroused, will compel you to watch out for illustrated articles about the Holy Land and to keep postcards from there. A map of the Holy Land will soon prove to be an absolute must. What fun it was when we also found a map of Vermont on the same scale and put the two on the wall next to each other to compare. The distance from Nazareth to Bethlehem was about as far as from Stowe to Rutland, or a little less. From Jerusalem to Bethlehem it would be five miles south of Stowe and one mile east. It is a good idea to take a family hike of just this distance once, both ways on foot, of course, because soon we accompany the Holy Family on their way to Jerusalem, to the temple.

"The days of her purifying" refers to a law in the Old Testament. "She shall touch no hallowed thing," it says of a mother after she has given birth to a child, "nor come into the sanctuary, until the days of her purifying be fulfilled" (Lev. 12:4;KJV). This was 40 days if the child was a boy and 80 days if the child was a girl, that the mother could not enter the temple and was liturgically unclean. Then the law continues: "And when the days of her purification are fulfilled, for a son, or for a daughter, she shall bring a lamb of the first year for a burnt offering, and a young pigeon, or a turtledove, for a sin offering, unto the door of the tabernacle of the congregation, unto the priest: Who shall offer it before the LORD, and make an atonement for her; and she shall be cleansed. . . . And if she be not able to bring a lamb, then she shall bring two turtles, or two young pigeons . . . and the priest shall make an atonement for her, and she shall be clean" (Lev. 12:6-8;KJV). Right away the idea comes to one's mind: Mary was not allowed to touch any holy thing — but there she was carrying holiness itself around in her arms, and she was not supposed to enter into the sanctuary of the temple.

After the purification of the mother there was still another law to fulfill, and that was the presentation of the boy: "And the Lord spake unto Moses, saying, Sanctify unto me all the firstborn, whatsoever openeth the womb among the children of Israel, [both] of man and of beast: it [is] mine" (Exod. 13:1–2;KJV).

This law served as a reminder to the Jews that God had once slain the Egyptians and taken their firstborn sons but had spared the firstborn of the Hebrews. Now in order that the child might go back home with his parents and not to have to remain in the temple for the service of the Lord, the parents had to pay a certain sum in silver — about five dollars in our money — as ransom money. This was the law for 11 of the 12 tribes of Israel. The sons of the tribe of Aaron, however, were destined to the priesthood. No money had to be paid for them. So Jesus' little cousin John, belonging to the tribe of Aaron, did not fall under that law. Jesus, belonging to the tribe of Judah, did.

One of the great beauties of reading through the Gospels like this is that after doing it a while, it will very often happen that the passage you are reading will bring to mind another one. Young minds are especially keen at finding such apropos comparisons. Therefore, having worked on "the days of her purification," one of the family might muse, "But Mary had been greeted by the angel, 'Hail, O favored one.' Didn't she know that the birth of this child couldn't possibly make her liturgically unclean? And then — the same angel has said to her, 'He . . . will be called the Son of the Most High; and the Lord God will give to him the throne of his father David . . . and of his kingdom there will be no end' (Luke 1:28–33). Didn't she feel within herself that this Son would not have to be bought with ransom money?"

And the family circle decides that she must have known. But in her actions she now accepted what her Son would later express in words to His cousin the Baptist when he didn't want to baptize Him, but would rather have been baptized by Him: "Let it be so now; for thus it is fitting for us to fulfil all righteousness" (Matt. 3:15).

A few years ago we were talking about this same subject, and again we came to the point that our Lord really

didn't *have* to follow the law, when young Rosmarie remarked, "Well, isn't this exactly like the story with the income tax?" (It was February, on the Feast of the Presentation, and the phrase "income tax" must have been heard
frequently around the house.)

"Which story with the income tax?" We asked, somewhat dumbfounded.

"Oh," said Rosmarie, "wasn't our Lord once reminded
that He hadn't paid His tax yet, and didn't He say to Peter,
His friend, pretty clearly that He didn't have to?" Fever-
ishly turning the pages in her New Testament, she had
found the place (Matt. 17:24-26) and read it to us trium-
phantly. "What do you think, Simon? From whom do kings
of the earth take toll or tribute? From their sons or from
others?" (Matt. 17:25).

In her own words she continued, "And Peter would
say, 'From others, of course.' " Then returning to the Book:
" 'Then the sons are free. However, not to give offense to
them, go to the sea and cast a hook, and take the first fish
that comes up, and when you open its mouth you will find
a shekel; take that and give it to them for me and for yourself' " (Luke 17:26–27).

It is a real feast if oneself or someone in the family
finds such connections as the "story of the income tax."
So, it is pretty safe to say that of course, Mary knew, but
"that we may not give offense to them," she prepared for
the three-fold ceremonies: her purification, the presentation
of the Son, and the sacrifice for sin.

Pitilessly the children want to know: "What happened
in those weeks before they went to the temple?"

The Gospel doesn't say. No contemporary of those
days is still living, no photographs were taken, no diaries
were kept. But it must have happened *somehow*, and in all
reverence, my guess is as good as yours. For instance, Ain

Karim, the home of Zacharias and Elizabeth, was only about a mile and a half away from Bethlehem in the hill country. Isn't it more than likely that within these 40 days of waiting Elizabeth would show up and repay the visit of her young cousin? Most probably she would bring Zacharias and her baby boy. How much rejoicing there would be among the two families!

We don't know anything about the parents of Mary, but tradition has it that their names were Joachim and Anna. Down to the earliest times of Christianity, artists have pictured Anna as a happy grandmother with her daughter Mary and her little grandson. Couldn't it be that some people from Nazareth returning from the census in Bethlehem brought the message to Anna that the baby had arrived, and her daughter and son-in-law would wait those 40 days near Jerusalem? What would any mother in our day think and do in such a case? She would exclaim: "Oh, my poor girl! She only took the most necessary things for emergency with her. I must get her everything she could possibly need." And then the elderly woman might start out on the trip herself, impatient to see the precious grandchild.

Sure, this is all "might be" and "maybe," but if I want to bring those 40 days of waiting to life, I certainly must use all my God-given faculties: the intellect and the memory for studying, and imagination, to be applied lovingly to reading between the lines. If we only consider what a part imagination plays in public life, in the world of fiction writing, movies, radio, and television! It couldn't possibly be put to better use than to help us to perceive how He did what He did, or what He looked like when He said certain things. It seems as if only the painters have made use of this privilege "to figure it all out." When we think of the "annunciations," the "visitations," and the "nativities" as they were imagined by painters and sculptors throughout the centuries, it should serve as a stimulus to our imagination. "All right, that's the way Giotto or Raphael, Michelangelo or Albrecht Durer saw it. Which way would you and I picture it?" And isn't it a shame that you and I would most probably have to admit that we hadn't gotten around yet to thinking about it, and just took Raphael and Fra Angelico and their pitiful descendants from Barclay Street and St. Sulpice as substitutes.

It is said that in the fourth century the market women in Constantinople were throwing cabbage heads at each other because they had different opinions about the Most Holy Trinity. Isn't it rather sad that we have to admit that while market women might still throw cabbage heads at each other, the reasons for doing so have changed so completely! Who cares now, for instance, what happened to Jesus, Mary, and Joseph while they were waiting for the days of her purification to be fulfilled?

Finally the morning of the great feast day dawned. Mary and Joseph must have set out with the child very early that morning to be in time for the morning sacrifice in the temple, after which the mothers used to be purified.

They were nearing her second home now — the temple. Tradition tells us that Mary had been brought to the house of God when she was three years old. As a temple virgin she spent her whole youth within the holy walls of the cloister together with other young girls from the first families. It was the highest education a young woman in Israel could get. They were taught how to read and write. If we consider that all boys had to learn to read (only the boys, not the girls), but not how to write, we understand what a privilege it was to be a temple virgin. They were instructed in Holy Scriptures, some of which, like the Psalms and the Proverbs, they had to learn by heart. They were taught how to cook and took turns cooking for the priests. They learned how to spin and weave and embroider. Is it any wonder that they were the most sought-after brides in Israel? The temple, besides being the house of the Most High, was for Mary also her home, her alma mater. The fondest memories of her youth were connected with it. Only a year or two had she been away from this sacred place, but how much had happened to her in that short time. First her espousal to Joseph, then the earthshaking moment of the annunciation. Her visit with Elizabeth, maybe the happiest months of her life; then the heart-rending weeks when she witnessed Joseph's worries. The trip down to Bethlehem, the mystery of the Holy Night, the shepherds and their story about the angels. Now here she was back at the temple — not alone, but with her husband and her son, pondering in her heart the great things said to her by the angel and by Elizabeth.

The temple — how much do we know about it — its shape, size, cervices, porches, gates, courts, and priests? For our Lord it will always be the house of the Father. It will be said of Him in the words of the Sixty-ninth Psalm: "Zeal for thy house will consume me" (John 2:17). One day He will cleanse it in vigor and wrath. Of the last days of His life it is said, "And he was teaching daily in the temple" (Luke 19:47). Just how familiar are we with it? Most of us do not give it a second thought and take the temple simply for something like a big church. How astonished we are, therefore, when we find out that at that time the temple occupied a square of more than 950 feet. This would make it more than half again as long at St. Peter's in Rome, which measures 613 feet.

During recent excavations of the temple, stones have been found measuring from 20 to 40 feet in length and weighing about one hundred tons. In the back of the large confraternity edition of the New Testament is a colored plan which gives us an idea. Soon we find ourselves hunting for pictures and more information and, if possible, a scale model. They are very rarely to be found, though, so why not make one yourself? It is exciting and interesting.

There are whole books written on the temple, one by Alfred Edersheim: *The Temple, Its Ministry and Services as They Were in the Time of Christ.* In a book by Father O'Shea, *Mary and Joseph, Their Life and Times,* are three very helpful chapters on the temple: "The Priests of Jehovah," "The House of Jehovah," and "The Hour of Incense."[1] If, after some study, we try to reconstruct the temple on a small scale with our girls and boys — must not Our Lord be pleased that we show so much interest in the house of the Father so dear to His heart? After having worked with cardboard, paper, and glue for weeks that way, we shall find ourselves richly rewarded, because we don't feel like strangers any more.

We understand better when we read together the following passages in the New Testament: "Then the devil took him to the holy city, and set him on the pinnacle of the temple" (Matt. 4:5). "Zechariah the son of Barachiah, whom you murdered between the sanctuary and the altar" (Matt. 23:35). "And throwing down the pieces of silver in the temple" (Matt. 27:5). "Two men went up into the temple to pray" (Luke 18:10). "Day after day I was with you in the temple teaching" (Mark 14:49). "And behold the curtain of the temple was torn in two, from top to bottom" (Matt. 27:51). "The one who sat for alms at the Beautiful Gate of the temple" (Acts 3:10).

We can closely accompany the Holy Family when they pass through the royal gate entering the temple. First they walked through the royal cloisters, a hall bigger than any Christian basilica has ever been , a richly carved roof carried by 162 beautiful pillars a hundred feet high. There were benches for everyone who wanted to rest. This was the place for all the beggars and the blind and deaf and dumb and those afflicted with many sicknesses, all of them exhibiting their troubles to move the charity of the many passers-by. At the time there were no hospitals in Jerusalem, and no board of social welfare.

After they had passed the covered cloister, the Holy Family stepped out into the vast Court of the Gentiles. Here were the tables of the moneychangers and the temple markets. As pilgrims came to Jerusalem from every nation under heaven, they were forced to change their foreign currency into the temple coins. A long story could be told about the temple markets and all the crooked business going on there. That's where Mary and Joseph bought the two turtledoves because they were so poor they could not afford to buy a lamb. Mary carried her child, and Joseph carried the turtledoves and the money. They went across the vast open court up to the barrier, a wall about four feet high bearing inscriptions in Greek telling the Gentiles to go no further under penalty of death. But Mary and Joseph were allowed by the guards to pass.

The real temple buildings were rising before them now. Up a flight of 15 steps they came to the gate called "Beautiful," which was 80 feet high and 30 feet wide, made of heavy Corinthian bronze. The Holy Family approached the Court of the Women. There were many halls and latticed galleries. Crossing through, they came to another splendid gate called Nicanor. Outside this gate, which was made of silver and gold, they had to wait until they heard the silver trumpets blow. This was the sign of the closing of the morning sacrifice. Now the mothers to be purified lined up on the steps. And Mary the mother of Jesus was there, too. Through the golden bars she could see the huge altar from which clouds of incense rose, and behind it the tremendous façade of the house of God. If Mary looked, she could see through the open door the magnificent veil. Perhaps her own hands helped to weave it. The other women standing there with Mary on that morning must have gazed with awe at the veil behind which was the Holy of Holies. Nobody paid any special attention to the most beautiful of the mothers waiting there — not the other women, not the 50 priests around the altar, not the guards of the temple police. Nobody knew that the God of Israel had really come to His house this morning — in the arms of the beautiful maiden.

Now the deep tones of the great organ called the Magraphah were to be heard. The white—robed priests came to accept the doves for the sin offering. The birds were taken in, killed, some of the blood spilling on the altar, and their flesh had to be eaten by the priests on the grounds of the temple. Some of the birds were burned, and the ceremony of the purification was over. All the mothers had become liturgically clean again. After this came the ceremony of the presentation. Out of the group of women, only the mothers with first-born sons approached the priest, presenting the baby to him.

Two blessings were spoken: one in thanksgiving for the birth of a son, and the other had to do with the law of ransom. The five shekels were handed over to the priest, and the ceremony was finished. It was finished for all the mothers except one. When Mary went down the steps to meet Joseph and they both were just about to disappear humbly in the great stream of worshipers, they were stopped by a venerable old man. It was Simeon, of whom it is said that: "This man was righteous and devout, looking for the consolation of Israel, and the Holy Spirit was upon him" (Luke 2:25). By the inspiration of the Spirit he came into the temple. He had been waiting at the foot of the steps watching the women coming down, all young mothers proud and happy. When he saw the most beautiful, the most radiant of them all, the Holy Ghost revealed to him that the beautiful little child in her arms was the Son of God. This was the most sublime moment of his long life. He approached her and stretched his arms out. Looking into the old face, she handed the child to him. What emotions must have filled the heart of the old man when he pressed his infant Savior to his heart, breaking out into the canticle of joy, "*Nunc dimittis. . . .*" "And his father and his mother marveled at what was said about him; and Simeon blessed them and said to Mary his mother, 'Behold, this child is set for the fall and rising of many in Israel, and for a sign that is spoken against (and a sword will pierce through your own soul also), that thoughts out of many hearts may be revealed' " (Luke 2:33–35). He handed back the child to His mother, who received Him in deep silence, pondering over this terrible prophecy.

Then before they could turn around to go home, there came an old lady, a widow of 84 years. She must have been in the temple during Mary's time, because it says of her that she "did not depart from the temple, worshiping with fasting and prayer night and day" (Luke 2:37). Old Anna had also been told the secret by the Holy Ghost. That's why she came up that very hour and began to give praise to the Lord. Then she turned around and "spoke of him to all who were looking for the redemption of Jerusalem" (Luke 2:38). One can't help asking: "And who were those?" Obviously they were none of the great ones in the temple, the mighty and powerful ones, because nothing at all happened. The Holy Family quietly left the house of God.

What must have been going on in Mary's heart? She knew that she was the mother of the Messiah. As a temple virgin she had learned all the messianic prophecies by heart, and from the Twenty-first Psalm she knew the horrible fate that awaited the One who would redeem His people. But maybe she hoped that the Heavenly Father might change His mind, as He had done with Nineveh when He had sent the prophet Jonas into the town with the strict message that Nineveh was to be destroyed. Then when He saw the repentance and good will of the people, He forgave and Nineveh was not destroyed. Well, if Mary had ever had such hopes for the future of her Son, Simeon had destroyed them. While they were walking back to their humble home in Bethlehem in deep silence meditating on what had happened, the sword of which he had spoken had already begun to pierce her soul.

"Mother, and what does that mean, 'That, out of many hearts, thoughts may be revealed'?" asks one of the children. Yes — what does that mean?

Years have passed since that question was asked. At least once a year we meditate on this part of the Gospels, and we are still pondering this question in our hearts.

Chapter 8

Caspar, Melchior, and Balthasar

It was a few years ago, and a wonderful winter day. I had been working with Hester, my secretary, in my little house, which is halfway up the hill behind the big house, and after a quick supper in the main house, had returned there to work. We had just admired one of our gorgeous mountain sunsets and were about to light the kerosene lamp when I saw something coming up the slope. It looked as if a big yellow star were climbing up the hill.

Hester and I went out onto the porch, and now we saw that we had visitors. In the deep snow, those colorful but quaintly dressed figures looked very much like foreigners. The first one was on horseback, and the star kept right above him, while the other two had a hard time wading through the knee-deep snow. One of them swung a censer, and the sweet fragrance of incense filled the crisp winter air. Finally they arrived, and lining up, enveloped in pungent clouds, they sang:

65

> We three kings of Orient are,
> Bearing gifts we traverse afar
> Field and fountain, moor and mountain,
> Following yonder star.
> Oh-h, star of wonder, star of light. . . .

At this moment Peanuts, the pony, had to sneeze. He wasn't used to incense. While the holy kings were singing beautifully and clearly in three parts, I recognized my two best brocade aprons acting as Turkish trousers on the legs dangling from Peanuts. I had a pretty good suspicion that they belonged to little Johannes, but was not quite sure yet. His countenance was dark black, and so was the little fist holding the stick with the star, a masterpiece consisting of transparent paper, cardboard, a flashlight battery and bulb, and the longest broomstick in the house. The other two royalties were dressed in the best silk curtains from the living and dining rooms, and wore the most beautiful golden crowns on their heads. His black majesty was wearing a white turban under his crown, a very becoming contrast to his complexion.

I know now without looking at the calendar that it must be January 5. These were the "Star Singers" (*Sternsaenger*), an old Austrian custom going back through the centuries. On the evening of the Epiphany the children dress up as the three holy kings and go from house to house singing. There is only one great difference between the original holy kings and their little imitators: The first ones brought gifts, the others expect them. They get apples and oranges, dried figs and prunes, cookies and candies, and sometimes also a little money. I felt very much embarrassed at being caught unawares and asked Hester in a whisper whether we had anything in that line in our little study. We didn't, so I quickly invented paper money of my own, worth fifty cents each, which could be cashed in Father Wasner's room. The grateful little kings — Ili, Lorli, and Johannes, our three youngest ones — sang a thank-you song, through which Peanuts impatiently and understandably pawed the ground. According to the color of his king, he must have come from Africa and was not accustomed to our Vermont winters. Then in majesty and dignity they descended the hill "following yonder star."

Meanwhile, the real stars had come out, and the thin sickle of the new moon was hanging in the ink-blue sky over Stowe Hollow. Traces of incense were still around us, and it had all been so poetic and a little unreal that Hester and I stood and watched until the big yellow star had disappeared among the old apple trees and the young voices were trailing off. Only now did we notice how cold it was, and went back in to our little wood stove. The kerosene lamp, however, was not lit that whole evening.

Hester, who had not known this folk custom, found it very lovely and said musingly, "How much does one really know about the story of the three holy kings?"

Well, this has been foremost among our research projects for many a Christmas, so I told her what we had discovered. "Now when Jesus was born in Bethlehem of Judea in the days of Herod the king, behold, wise men from the East came to Jerusalem, saying, 'Where is he who has been born king of the Jews? For we have seen his star in the East, and have come to worship him' " (Matt. 2:1–2).

Who were those wise men from the East? Since the third century, going back to Tertullian, there is a tradition which calls them "Magi" and "kings." This fits perfectly with the psalm which says, "May the kings of Tarshish and of the isles render him tribute, may the kings of Sheba and Seba bring gifts!" (Ps. 72:10). Among the old Medes and Persians such Magi were known, a very exclusive caste who led strict lives and kept the fire going at their places of worship in the mountains and studied the stars of heaven and the dreams of men. These men must have heard of the prophecy, "A star shall come forth out of Jacob and a sceptre shall rise out of Israel" (Num. 24:17).

The Jews, who had been led into captivity several times, had spread the knowledge of a coming Messiah all over the Orient and deep into Persia, where the adventure of Tobias and Esther had taken place. The only thing the Gospel of Matthew tells us about the three high personages is that they were wise men and came from the Orient. Now also from the Orient come many legends and stories. One such story says that the Magi were descendants of the great Balaam. The golden coins they brought to little Jesus had been coined by Terah, the father of Abraham, and Joseph, the son of Jacob. It is interesting that the Gospel doesn't talk about the number, how many there were, but in all pictures and pieces of sculpture there are always three. Some people say they represent the three ages of men: youth, maturity, and old age. Others say they are the representatives of different races: the Semitic, the Caucasian, and the Negro. People gave them the names of Caspar, Melchior, and Balthasar. An old Christian tradition says that Thomas baptized them on his way to India, and now their relics are venerated in the Cathedral of Cologne.

How much can one find out about the star? There are many hypotheses. One says it must have been a comet, another says it was a newly appearing star, again another one thinks it was not a star at all, but a strong light like the lights of the Zodiac, which are frequently visible in the Orient. These and many other theories of a more learned nature have been used to explain the words, "We have seen his star in the east."

The Church has not decided on any one of these details, so we in our family have settled on this story. We are all descended from Noah and his family: "The sons of Noah who went forth from the ark were Shem, Ham, and Japheth. . . . and from these the whole earth was peopled" (Gen. 9:18–19). Caucasians descended from Japheth; the people of the Middle East and Asia descended from Shem; and the Africans from Ham. The story that we like best is this: In Ethiopia, in Persia, and far away in the Caucasus, wise men were watching the sky for a special star which was promised to mankind. On one and the same day they all saw it appear and decided independently of each other, not even knowing of each other, to go and adore the new-born King whose sign the star had been. It took them many months to prepare a caravan worthy of royalty. When their plan became known, they were warned against their undertaking and finally ridiculed.

After starting on their way, it took them many more months, and finally one blessed day they were brought *together* by the star in the desert. Now they traveled the last stretch of their journey *together* until at last they saw the high mountains of Moab appearing on the horizon. These were the mountains which Balaam, the great ancestor of all Magi, climbed up with the intention of cursing the people of Israel, and instead he blessed them. These are the mountains on whose peak Moses had stood in silence gazing into the Promised Land which he was not allowed to enter. From these mountains of Moab, the Magi looked down into this canyon which is the Jordan Valley.

Now they knew they were near the end of their journey. How much time had they spent on the road? We don't know, but each one had come a tremendous distance, and the caravans of old made about 10 or 12 miles a day. When they approached the Jordan, their animals must have drunk greedily after having crossed the desert. They came into

Jericho, which had been just newly rebuilt by King Herod. The boundaries of the Roman Empire were there, and customs officers must have searched their rich caravans. Now they were really on the way to Jerusalem. It was that feared stretch of wild countryside infested with robbers, but a strong party such as theirs did not have to worry. Soon they were in the hills of Judea, and finally they saw the walls of the Holy City and the temple of stone and gold rising above it.

They entered through the city gate and asked the first person they met, "Where is he who has been born king of the Jews? For we have seen his star in the East, and have come to worship him" (Matt. 2:2). This question was overheard by the Gestapo.

"By whom?" asked Hester, who had been listening in rapt attention, but who couldn't fit this modern word into our ancient oriental story. The spell was broken, and now we could just as well feed our little stove before it grew cold.

"Matthew continues," I said to Hester, "When Herod the king heard this, he was troubled, and all Jerusalem with him" (Matt. 2:3)

From all I have read and learned about King Herod, he reminds me very much of Hitler and, coming from an invaded country where one had to beware of the Gestapo who, as the saying went, "heard the grass grow," I understand how all Jerusalem was troubled. This Herod had not a drop of Jewish blood in his veins. His father was a Bedouin from Idumea, and his mother an Arabian princess. Of course, he was no descendant of David. He had gotten to the throne by kowtowing to the Romans. When they finally made him king of the Jews, they little knew that they were fulfilling the prophecy: "The scepter shall not depart from Judah . . . until he comes to whom it belongs; and to him shall be the obedience of the peoples" (Gen. 49:10).

In order to make it look a little better, Herod married Mariamne, the granddaughter of the last real priest, King Hyrcanus. Her family was very little pleased about this, and so he simply began to liquidate them. He killed old Hyrcanus and Alexandra his daughter, Mariamne's mother. Mariamne herself was the only being he ever really loved in his life, but one day in a fit of jealousy, he killed her with his own hands. Then he drowned his brother-in-law, the young high priest Aristobulos, because he got too popular for Herod's taste. Soon afterward his own two sons were strangled in the bath. When Herod was already very sick, he had his third son beheaded.

No wonder his subjects hated him! By and by he had built up such an efficient system of secret police that whatever happened in Jerusalem he knew of within five minutes. Exactly like the Gestapo. Therefore, when those harmless strangers asked for the newborn King, we can understand how all of Jerusalem was troubled because this was the feared word Herod could not stand. During the time of his reign there had been much bloodshed — mass massacre as well as single murders. A rumor had swept throughout the city that Herod, who was by now dying, had arranged in his last will that immediately upon his death a mass murder was to take place. All the leading men in the nation were to be killed, in order that there might be tears shed in the Jewish nation on the day of his death.

"You see, Hester," I said, "it must have been pretty similar in the little country of the Jews to our own small Austria. Both had been invaded, and were ruled by Quislings, and both had a Gestapo — the fear of which takes a long, long time to get out of your bones. Therefore, I can so very well understand what the Evangelist meant when he said, 'When Herod the king heard this, he was troubled, and all Jerusalem with him' (Matt. 2:3)."

Who is going to be killed next? was the question everyone turned over in his mind. Then the Gospel continues: "And assembling all the chief priests and the scribes of the people, he inquired of them where the Christ was to be born" (Matt. 2:4).

The news must have reached Herod in an incredibly short time that this big, rich caravan with very strange-looking foreigners had entered Jerusalem. Immediately he summoned the Sanhedrin, and the 72 members would have obeyed the royal call immediately because it is not safe to delay when a Hitler calls. Everyone in the city must have held his breath, and the 72 dignified elders must have wondered if they were going to leave the palace alive.

When they were admitted into the presence of the king, they salaamed until their beards touched the ground. When they were finished with the ceremonial bows and glanced at the face of their king, the Jews could read there that Herod was troubled. When he glared at them in contempt — that is all he ever had for his Jewish subjects, he the great admirer of the Greeks — there must have been an almost unbearable tension in the room: *What does he want of us? What is he going to do now?*

When he finally snapped the question, "Where is the Christ born?" with an almost unbelieving sigh of relief they broke out with the answer — not only a spokesman, but "they" said to him, says the Gospel, "In Bethlehem of Judea, for so it is written by the prophet" (Matt. 2:5). And then they quoted the age-old prophecy of Micah as of one voice: "O Bethlehem Ephrathah . . . from you shall come forth for me one who is to be ruler in Israel" (Mic. 5:2).

That was all. He didn't want to hear any more. They were dismissed. It must have been almost too good to be true for them. And now the dying tyrant was thinking fast. Other messengers went out to summon the illustrious strangers. The Gospel goes on "Then Herod summoned the wise men secretly and ascertained from them what time the star appeared" (Matt. 2:7).

What a different company now appeared before King Herod! Not the submissive subjects of a dictator, always trembling in their boots, but free men, kings greeting a king. There was salaaming again, but this time it was on both sides, and the sick man on his golden couch tried very, very hard to be at his best. His shrewd, wicked mind was all made up. At his earliest opportunity he had to do away with that "King of the Jews" whom these magnificent-looking foreigners had come to adore, but first he must find out something about Him. They had said they had seen His star. Very much depended now on the time. Herod feared that the star might have appeared to them many years ago, and this King of the Jews, the Messiah, might be a warrior now, ready to strike. That is why Herod "ascertained from them what time the star appeared." What a sigh of relief when he learned the time! An ugly smile played around his cruel lips when he thought that his opponent was a mere baby in His mother's arms. But he had to finish his act, and he played it well. "And he sent them to Bethlehem, saying, 'Go and search diligently for the child, and when you have found him bring me word, that I too may come and worship him' " (Matt. 2:8).

With childlike minds, they bowed and assured him that of course nothing would give them more pleasure; and with this promise the venerable men hurried to meet their caravan to be on the way, now that they knew where to go. "Wise men," the Gospel calls them, but Herod had outsmarted them, so it seemed, because "the sons of this world are more shrewd in dealing with their own generation than the sons of light" (Luke 16:8).

"When they had heard the king they went their way; and lo, the star which they had seen in the East went before them, till it came to rest over the place where the child was. When they saw the star, they rejoiced exceedingly with great joy" (Matt. 2:9–10).

After not having seen the star for a while, they now view it with great joy. Only now can we imagine what a terrific trial Jerusalem must have been to those kingly souls. After their great decision to come all those vast distances, after the preparations and troubles and dangers of the journey, they finally reached the goal, the capital of the land of the Jews and the palace of the king, where, of course, they expected the Infant to be.

When they saw the perplexity on everybody's faces when they asked the eager question, "Where is the newborn King of the Jews?" they grew more and more puzzled, and even the star had disappeared. Maybe this was the darkest hour in their lives. If the people at home had perhaps been startled at their whole undertaking, every word of their warning must have come back now when it all seemed to be a failure. It is so very humanly possible that the temptation may have arisen to leave quietly before their embarrassing situation became too widely known. They must have felt ashamed and embarrassed and bitterly disappointed when they learned that for a long, long time there hadn't been a baby born in this royal palace of Jerusalem. But they were too unsophisticated and truly great just to leave quickly, turn the heads of their camel towards the east and vanish into the Syrian Desert. They believed in the star and in the One who had sent it, even after it had disappeared, and now — what a royal reward!

The moon had left Stowe Hollow and was now standing directly over Cor Unum, our house. On account of the snow all around us, there was a dim twilight in the room — and a deep silence.

"And?" said Hester finally.

"Oh, excuse me," I replied. "I couldn't help thinking of the time when our family felt some of this 'exceeding great joy.' That was when in our life the star reappeared, too."

Hester looked at me, and it was bright enough to see the questioning expression on her face, although she didn't say anything. So I explained. "One day in our life as a family we saw a great big light just as the kings saw the star. It was the time when we saw clearly that we had to give up our material goods in order to save the spiritual ones; and as an entire family — father, mother, and nine children — leave our native Austria and become voluntary refugees. The few friends and relatives who heard about this were aghast and very much against it. When we finally, after many adventures, reached our Jerusalem, namely New York City, thinking now we had reached the goal, it looked all of a sudden like a complete failure. The star was gone. In our hearts resounded the words of our well-meaning friends about Hitler's promise of a thousand years of peace and the brilliant future our children could have had in his Third Reich — and there we were in America and nobody seemed to want us. It was a very dark hour. The war with Germany had not yet broken out. People urged us to go back; we could never be a success in this country. I shall never forget that particular hour. We were in the Hotel Wellington, my husband and I. It was past midnight and a gentleman had just left who for hours had tried to persuade us to go home on the next boat. When the door had closed behind him, I looked at my husband. We were both tired and very much discouraged. We had just enough money left to pay for our hotel, and there didn't seem to be any future.

"Then Georg said, 'We were so deeply convinced when we left Salzburg that this was the will of God, and when one day we came through Cologne and knelt at the shrine of the three holy kings, we made them our patron saints for the time of our wanderings. Then we promised God to imitate them and persevere even if we couldn't see the star. I think this is the time now.'

"Still very tired, but not desperate any more, we went to bed. And then it all happened fast. We found the manager who understood us and in whose hands we felt safe as artists as well as people. 'And lo, the star which they had seen in the East went before them, till it came to rest over the place where the child was. When they saw the star, they rejoiced exceedingly with great joy.'

"You see," I concluded my little digression, "the Gospel is still going on in our very own days, and if we only would let Him, our Lord would re-live His life in each one of our lives all over again. Don't you know from your own past the times when the star has seemingly vanished, and don't you know this 'exceeding great joy' when it appears again?"

"I think I know what you mean," said Hester, and she seemed to know what she was talking about. "And?" she added, which made me conscious that I hadn't finished my story of the three holy kings yet.

It must have been rather late by now, because, in the house below, one after another of the lighted windows was darkened. "Let's not look at the watch, but let's finish," I resolved.

When they had passed through the city gate, they had to go directly south for five miles. This is something for our imagination to dwell on: the long caravan, really three caravans merged in one, the many camels with their bells, the swift horses, the stately elephants — for each king had come on the animals of his country — and a big star traveling above them in the air, enveloping them all in a soft light. How they must all have looked up to the star gliding along before them and thanked God from the depths of their hearts. After five miles the road turned sharply to the left, and there they saw Bethlehem, the little town perched on the hillside — like Assisi — in the midst of vineyards and olive groves, surrounded by big sheep pastures. The star traveled right into town and stopped above a house.

There was no doubt: now they had reached their destination. Camels and elephants dropped to their knees, horses stood still, and the next moment the Magi-kings had dismounted and were now beckoning to their servants. This was a sign which they understood well, and the kings were brought the gifts which were intended for the newborn King of the Jews. In the East it was the custom to give a present to any superior as a sign of respect. We see that repeatedly in the Old Testament. Now Matthew tells us, "Then, opening their treasures, they offered him gifts, gold and frankincense and myrrh" (Matt. 2:11).

On this very day Joseph must not have been at home. He was most probably at work somewhere because "they found the child with Mary his mother." And now something quaint happens: "They fell down and worshiped him." Little Jesus was obviously sitting on His mother's lap. And His mother, the most humble handmaid of the Lord, accepted the homage of these venerable men with complete composure. She did not stop them. She did not interrupt their adoration with polite words. She knew that falling down and prostrating was a tribute given only to God, and Mary accepted it for the little King.

Later, our Lord would exclaim several times: "Truly . . . not even in Israel have I found such faith" (Matt. 8:10), always talking about one or another Gentile. If the little Child could have talked, He would have said the same right then. The Sanhedrin, the official law-giving body, had formally announced that "the Christ is to be born in Bethlehem," and everybody understood that this little Child the highborn strangers from the Orient had come to worship must be identical with Him. It is one of the greatest riddles that the members of the Sanhedrin just seem to have returned to their homes from their summons to the king. No one — no Pharisee, Sadducee, rabbi, nor any of the elders — seems to have taken any action at all concerning the child only a few miles away in Bethlehem. Some of them must have heard some rumors of the birth in the cave with the manger, of the Gloria in Excelsius, or of the talk of Simeon and Anna. It is just incredible and unbelievable that nothing, absolutely nothing, was done until the pagans — the Gentiles — prostrated themselves before Him and presented Him with gifts.

St. Bede the Venerable says, "The first is said to have been Melchoir, a bald man with a long beard and hair, who offered gold to the King and Lord" (princes from the East always honored their sovereigns with a gift of gold). The second, Caspar, was a beardless young man of a ruddy hue, and he came with frankincense, the most expensive fragrance of the East, always considered too precious to use for humans, and always reserved for the temples. Then came Balthasar, the dark one. His vessel of myrrh reminds us of the story of his people, grand but sad, myrrh used for the embalming of the dead. Never again in His whole life will our Lord be offered gold or frankincense, but twice He will be offered myrrh: on the cross by the soldiers, and after His death, by Nicodemus. Strangely enough, His mother will receive it from Nicodemus, as she receives it now from Balthasar.

After the official homage was paid in prostration and presenting of gifts, Mary got up, I am sure, and showed her precious little child to her noble guests. Each one was allowed to take Him in his arms and look at His smiling little face. It must have been the happiest moment of their lives.

Then with their hearts full to the brim, they must have asked the mother questions. Mary will be asked questions by another Gentile later and will tell all the wondrous secrets to him who will put them down as the Gospel of Luke. Mary might have told these great and venerable souls the story of the annunciation and what the angel said, the story of the visitation and what Elizabeth said, the story of the nativity and what the shepherds said. Then it was time for her royal guests to leave.

What a horror to think that at the same time the old dying man in Jerusalem with one foot in the grave was already preparing his soldiers to kill this beautiful young boy, who was now clapping His little hands and having the time of His life!

When Joseph came home from work that evening, Mary told him about the wondrous happenings of the day and showed him the gifts. To the mind of the silent man must have come the words of Psalm 72: "May all kings fall down before him, all nations serve him!" (Ps. 72:11). And then although they didn't know it, they spent their last quiet evening for a long, long time to come. The little boy had been put to bed. Mary and Joseph went and looked at the gold, frankincense, and myrrh.

Caspar, Melchior, and Balthasar could hardly go to sleep with so much happiness throbbing in their hearts. When their tired eyes had closed in slumber, an angel of the Lord came to them with a message from on high: they were not to return to Herod.

What a consolation to us when the children of the world all around us are getting smarter all the time! In prayer time we say every Sunday, "For he will give his angels charge of you to guard you in all your ways. On their hands they will bear you up, lest you dash your foot against a stone" (Ps. 90:11–12).

One can't help wondering whether this angel, having given his message, turned right around and went over to "the house" where he also had to deliver a message.

Caspar, Melchior, and Balthasar would get up quietly, order their camp to be broken up quickly, and instead of going north to Jerusalem, they would head straight east, for the Jordan, and in a couple of hours be across the border out of the reach of Herod. The mysterious East would swallow them up.

Tradition has it that after the apostle Thomas had baptized them, they in turn tried to preach Christianity in their countries, but met with so much hostility that they soon died for their Lord and King. The early Christians venerated them as martyrs.

Now the moon was looking directly into our window.

"When we go to Europe next year," Hester asked, "shall we stop at Cologne?"

"Oh, let us hope so," I said, and we walked down through the deep snow. The house was all dark now. Only the moon and the stars had witnessed the story which had warmed our hearts for the last hours.

CHAPTER
9

THE FUGITIVE

In the beginning of this book I told "how it happened." "It" means that we as a family became so much interested in the life of Christ that we started to rebuild it for ourselves, to re-live it day by day. After a few years of doing this, and as we knew Him better and better, we began to feel very close to Him. Finally, He was not only a good friend; more and more He became like one of us — a member of our family. As it had all begun with my telling my crying little girl the story of the flight into Egypt, this story has always remained a favorite among us. We have tried ever so hard to collect all that is known about it, and on top of this, use our family imagination. By now it has grown like this:

While in Bethlehem the two little groups of three holy persons each, the Holy Family and the holy kings, finally fell into peaceful slumber, Herod in nearby Jerusalem was very restless. For one thing, he could not sleep because of the awful disease which was eating him up; but on this night something else kept him awake — the thought of his innocent little rival. With growing impatience he awaited the return of the three kings. These stargazers — would they never come?

Little did he know that just now in the middle of the night the course of those "stargazers" had been changed, and they were already on their way far from him. He, of course, had expected them back the same evening, maybe late at night, and now the hours were dragging on, and he worked himself more and more into one of his paroxysms of wrath. The mere idea that this hated child should escape him drove him into fury.

In the early dawn of morning he shouted his commands, which he had changed from murdering just one little boy living in a certain house, to killing every child up to two years, to be absolutely sure *He* was among them. Herod had three companies of mercenaries: Galatians, Thracians, and Teutons. On these brutal soldiers he could depend to execute any command, however bloody, even against the members of his own family. A stiff march of an hour and a half took them to Bethlehem, where they began at once to scatter. They searched the houses, butchering the baby boys in their mothers' arms. Before the little town had fully awakened to what had happened, the soldiers were already on their way back. The shrieks of the inconsolable mothers rose to heaven: "A voice was heard in Ramah, wailing and loud lamentation, Rachel weeping for her children" (Matt. 2:18).

How many little boys were killed? It is said that Bethlehem had a thousand inhabitants at that time. The number of births in a year was about 30. In two years, therefore, there would be 60; and if half of them were girls, it would leave 30 boys. In those times, however, there was quite a high rate of infant mortality, so maybe there were no more than 20.

The little bodies lay in their blood, while their parents were completely overwhelmed with grief.

Matthew finishes his story about the three wise men: "And being warned in a dream not to return to Herod, they departed to their own country by another way. Now when they had departed, behold, an angel of the Lord appeared to Joseph in a dream and said, 'Rise, take the child and his mother, and flee to Egypt, and remain there till I tell you; for Herod is about to search for the child, to destroy him'" (Matt. 2:12–13).

"When they had departed," the Gospel says, so obviously, Caspar, Melchior, and Balthasar first disappeared with their caravan and were swallowed up by the darkness of the night when the angel came to Joseph with the command, "Rise." This meant immediate danger. These words of the gospel might never have been so widely and so fully understood since they were written down, as they were by millions and millions of people all over Europe and all over the encroaching realm of the Iron Curtain: "The Communists are coming — arise and flee!" What Herod was to his time, a tyrant, Lenin and Stalin have been to our days. They all have one thing in common: They have no use for "the Christ." Now as then, they seek to destroy Him. Therefore, the angel goes also through our days, or rather nights, and the "arise and flee" is heard by millions. That is why our times seem perhaps closer than any of the 19 centuries to the very beginnings of Christianity. Whenever refugees are fleeing because their Christian faith is threatened — all over the highways and byways of Poland, Germany, Austria, Czechoslovakia, Hungary, in the Balkans, or in China — they never have to feel alone. In them our Lord Jesus Christ, the same yesterday as today, is still on His flight into Egypt.

Joseph, tired though he was from his day's work, must have been immediately wide awake upon hearing the word "Rise, take the child and his mother." With a heavy heart he wakened Mary, who was so peacefully asleep with her baby, trusting so completely in his protection. When Mary recognized his voice and understood what he said, she arose — I almost said hastily, but no, that would not be right. I am absolutely sure that in her whole life she never did anything hastily. Everything she did and the very way she did it must always have been just right because she was so completely anchored in God. She just rose quickly, very quickly. And the handmaid of the Lord kept her head again as she had done when the great angel appeared in Nazareth, when Elizabeth had said such outstanding things, and when Simeon's message tore her heart. In no time she had wrapped up the little boy tenderly and taken the few things she would need, for poverty doesn't take long to pack. The only really valuable things they owned were the gifts of the kings. Joseph must have wrapped them carefully. Maybe in less than ten minutes they had quietly left the house. The donkey they came on from Nazareth must still have been around. And Joseph lifted Mary with the sleeping child in her arms on its back.

We feel it now as a great privilege to have been refugees once, to know what anxiety means. The clatter of the donkey's hooves on the cobblestones of Bethlehem, for instance: wouldn't that wake up somebody who might report them later? That's why they hurried down the slope into the vineyards and fields to get away as fast as possible. Every sound arouses ones fears. "Maybe they have found out and are on our heels" — that's the constant fear. When the sky grew light, the first cocks began to crow, and the horrid battalion entered the small town, perhaps Mary and Joseph, who were slow travelers, might still have heard the shrieks which rent the air and sent cold chills down their backs. They were still very close to Herod's power. They were still in the neighborhood where they might have been known and identified. . . .

Oh, it is so wrong to picture the flight into Egypt as a nice, smooth hike with angels on all sides ministering to them. The angels certainly were there admiring, adoring, almost unbelieving that the Lord would not have protected His only-begotten Son by means less troublesome than this pitiful flight. Where was the Angel of Death who slew the Egyptians? Where was the angel with the fiery sword at the gates of paradise? But it was obviously the will of the Most High that the Child and His mother be saved not by supernatural interference, but by the natural means of a tedious flight. We people living many centuries later understand perhaps a little better why: He really has become "like one of us," and we can go to Him also during a flight or a persecution, saying full of confidence, "You know how it is."

The books say that there were two main routes going from Judea into Egypt. It is interesting now to look them up on the map. The more popular route was "by way of the land of the Philistines" (Exod. 13:17), via Ascalon and Gaza and then along the shore of the Mediterranean towards the delta of the Nile. The other way led through Hebron and Beersheba to the land on the Nile. Every refugee will tell you that if one wants to get away from feared territory as quickly and safely as possible, one uses the less-traveled routes. That's why they must have gone south to Hebron about 15 miles. It has been ascertained that "the ordinary rate for a long journey on foot was about 17 Roman miles per day,"[1] so the Holy Family could have reached Hebron that first day. Every refugee will also tell you that you don't stay overnight in a town even if it should be dear to you because it contains the tomb of your own ancestors (like

Hebron, where Father Abraham had buried his beloved wife, Sarah); so they hurried on.

Farther south about 20 miles was an oasis, the famous Beersheba, the southernmost settlement in Judea. Did Mary and Joseph talk about the fact that from here Father Abraham had set out to sacrifice his only son, that here also he had pushed Hagar and Ishmael into the wilderness? Here Joseph must have filled their water bags, because now they were setting out into the barren desert. Beyond Beersheba they could afford to breathe a little more freely because they were out of Herod's immediate jurisdiction, but they were still in the Roman Province of Syria. You never could tell whether Herod had perhaps gotten the Romans to lend him a hand. Therefore, Mary and Joseph would keep hurrying on towards the river Rhinocolura. After having passed the frontier between Syria and Egypt, they did relax somewhat, but now came the worst stretch of the journey, more than a hundred miles of unbroken desert.

When we were on the way to California in our big blue bus, we saw for the first time in our lives real desert with sand dunes. Because of our favorite Gospel, we asked the driver to stop on the highway and we, taking our shoes and stocking off, waded into the dunes. We were thinking that the sandals of antiquity were not much more protection than going barefoot because the hot sand would be constantly between the soles and the leather. I remember so vividly how we couldn't stand it more than ten minutes, hastening back to the bus with a stinging sensation all over our legs which lasted the rest of the day. And this was in early spring, and the desert was not yet at its hottest. It certainly gave us firsthand experience of how those 360 miles between Bethlehem and Heliopolis must have been.

The books say that in those times little ones were nursed by their mothers for a full two years. Every mother knows that during the time of nursing one wants to drink a great deal. The water in the skins had to be dished out very sparingly. He, who would later feed five thousand and another time four thousand by a miracle, didn't do a thing to help himself or His mother and foster father, although a wave of His little hand would have turned the desert into paradise.

There are many lovely legends woven around this flight through the desert. Painters throughout the centuries have taken hold of them, and we see Mary resting peacefully on a green carpet of grass while Joseph is picking apples and the infant is playing with young lions. In another picture we see little Jesus beckoning to a group of tall date palms, they bending down so that He can pick what He wants, or the animals of the desert coming to their aid and the Holy Family riding on zebras, giraffes, and lions. The loveliest of all these stories, however, is the one true version that nothing extraordinary happened and they had to take every step through the hot sand by themselves, shiver through the cold nights, for us, for you and me. Since we discovered this story when we were just beginning as refugees, it warmed our hearts. It made us feel good in that company!

Finally, the weary wanderers saw before them the many waters of the Nile, the green and lush delta. Tradition has it that they went to Heliopolis. In order to get there they must have passed through many towns before, through well-irrigated fields, finally passing obelisks and pyramids. Mary and Joseph must have talked about the role Egypt had played in the history of their people. Abraham had fled there once in time of famine, and another Joseph had been taken there by force. At that Joseph's invitation he finally got his whole clan into the land. For the next four hundred years they would be first the guests of the pharaoh and later slaves until God would awaken Moses to lead them away into the

Promised Land. Mary and Joseph must have talked about all this, and many times they must have recited together the psalms which dealt with captivity and hardship and the Heavenly Father finally leading them out into green pastures.

One of the glories of doing this particular story from the Gospels as a family is that one really learns so much about Egypt. The different children in their different grades can now contribute what they know about the old Egyptians and how they lived. For the parents, school days are reawakened. One looks up old history books, and pooling it all, it is amazing what a good picture one can get of the Holy Family in Egypt! The most striking part of this story will be when it comes to the religion of the Egyptians. The books say that at the time of Christ the religion of the Egyptians had deteriorated into worshiping animals: crocodiles, snakes, birds, cows, cats, and rams, if they were born of one solid color. The books also say that many Jews had settled in Egypt, and in the big cities like Alexandria, Heliopolis, or Memphis, the population was about two-thirds Jewish. In Heliopolis there was a Jewish colony. That's where the Holy Family found refuge. Now they were in the true sense of the word "displaced persons" with no plans of their own, waiting to see what would be done with them. "Remain there," the angel had said, "till I tell you."

"If-ing it," or "perhaps-ing it" means, in our family, trying out different possible ways of how it might have been. "Perhaps," therefore, Joseph used the gold of Melchior to rent a house and get the necessary things to set up a humble household — this was never to be a home; this would always be exile.

Now Joseph would find himself work, and Mary would keep house. They were not rich enough to afford a baby sitter, so whenever she went shopping in the bazaar, she would take her little boy with her. It is perfectly possible that many a time she must have witnessed how the street crier came along making room for a sacred cow or a sacred cat, ordering everyone prostrate in the dust. Of course, Mary would never obey this command. The people would curse the Jewish swine, as they used to say in mockery, because the Jews did not touch any pork. There she stood pressed against the wall until the animals had slowly passed, holding by the hand Him who would someday exclaim, "I am the light of the world" (John 8:12). John also said "He was in the world, and the world was made through him, yet the world knew him not. He came to his own home, and his own people received him not" (John 1:10–11). Even if they were out of immediate danger from Herod, it must have made them very bitter to see how far the people around them had drifted away from God.

According to ancient tradition the Holy Family went from Heliopolis to Memphis and stayed there for the rest of the time. There those things must have happened which make the heart of every young mother warm with joy. At His mother's knee little Jesus would begin to talk and sing little songs. From her He was learning His first prayers and listening to His first stories. Now there is no end of "perhaps-ing." Which were His first words, which the first prayers, and what kind of stories? This depends a little bit on the question of how long the Holy Family stayed in Egypt. The fathers of the church are of different opinions. Bonaventure believed that they stayed in Egypt as long as seven years. Then the stories would most certainly be all those beautiful Bible stories, which in His case were at the same time family history. In the young heart would awaken homesickness for His Father's house, where the mother had dwelt for many years, and which she could describe so wonderfully. Like every refugee child, He would grow up on the stories of how it was in the "old country," which He himself could not remember because He was too small at the time of flight, but which filled His little heart with nostalgia.

Besides all hardships and all the nostalgia, there is one more emotion which fills the refugee's heart, and that is deep gratitude to his or her hosts for their hospitality. He wants to repay in whatever small measure he can. Christ repaid Egypt in His own inimitable hundred-fold ways: In the course of time its cities would be filled with bishops and saints, the wilderness around would swarm with the fathers of the desert. John Chrysostom would say of the Egypt of his own time in the fourth century: "And shouldst thou come now into the desert of Egypt, thou wilt see this desert become better than any paradise, and ten thousand choirs of angel in human forms, whole nations of martyrs and companies of virgins, and all the devil's tyranny put down while Christ's Kingdom shines forth in its brightness."

Every refugee is just living for the day when he can return home. Finally the glorious moment arrived when "Behold, an angel of the Lord appeared in a dream to Joseph in Egypt, saying, 'Rise, take the child and his mother, and go to the land of Israel, for those who sought the child's life are dead.' And he rose and took the child and his mother, and went to the land of Israel" (Matt. 2:19–21).

Upon this, invariably, one of the children will ask, "Why again at night? Why arise and take the child and His mother? Couldn't they just leave normally like any other travelers, join a caravan and have it a little easier?" Well, this is one of those questions to which we still have not found an answer.

One of our children asked once, "Mother if the three holy kings had to leave the same night, couldn't they have taken the Holy Family on their camels? Don't you think they would have enjoyed doing this, and just think how much easier for Mary and Joseph!" It had never occurred to me before, but it was a good suggestion, and there was no question of how they would have liked to do this. At least one of them had to go in that direction anyhow. The one from Ethiopia had to pass through Egypt to go home. The only answer is that the other was the will of the Heavenly Father.

How lighthearted they must have been on the long and hard journey back, reciting over and over again, "I was glad when they said to me, 'Let us go to the house of the Lord' " (Ps. 122:1). They were heading for Bethlehem. It might not be impossible that on one of these days the thought occurred to Mary that her little Jesus would have no playmates of His own age. The boys in Bethlehem would be either a little older or a little younger than He. Towards the very end of the trip, however, Joseph got another one of his nightly messages: He should not go to Bethlehem in Judea because the successor of Herod was not much better than Herod himself. Instead, he should go into Galilee. So they chose the hometown of the mother and went to Nazareth and settled there.

Maria von Trapp, shortly before the family's flight from Austria.

CHAPTER
10

"UNLESS YOU . . . BECOME LIKE CHILDREN"

A grave injustice is done to this family from Nazareth if we do not take them as real people; persons like you and me, completely alike in everything — except sin. For most of us, isn't Jesus — and I mean now humanly speaking — some kind of superman? And Mary, well — she is a myth, something of the same kind, very much to be admired but definitely not someone whom you would take into your home, whom you would ask to live with you, no more than you would invite a member of foreign royalty. You would feel too awkward, too uncomfortable. All the ease would be gone from your home, as if one couldn't smoke or relax in a chair in their presence; make small talk about the household, the high prices of nowadays, the threatening danger of war, as long as they are around. What a great, great pity, and how very wrong! Still

— isn't this the way it is with the majority of Christians nowadays? And why? Only because we don't know them.

What do we know, for instance, about the so-called "hidden life"? I dread this very expression "hidden life," because these two words seem to have had a strange influence on us. Most of the 30-some years of the life of Christ is covered by this expression which we have learned to accept as fact. Just because the Gospels don't say a word about what was going on in the Holy Family, we deprive ourselves of living His whole life with Him. The years of His childhood until He became of age as a "son of the law," the years from 12 to 20 when He had reached majority in His tribe, the precious years from 20 to 30 when He was a grown-up man like those in our families. But we people of today cannot do that any longer. There are books such as Bible encyclopedias in one volume or *Mary the Mother of Jesus* by Reverend Franz M. William or the books by Father O'Shea[1] and others which will help us reconstruct the daily life of the Holy Family almost as easily as we might reconstruct the daily life of our great-grandmothers.

Luke says, "They returned into Galilee, to their own city, Nazareth. And the child grew and became strong, filled with wisdom; and the favor of God was upon him" (Luke 2:39–40). And because nothing spectacular happened until He was 12 years old, there isn't anything more said but that they returned to Nazareth. The Evangelist might have felt foolish if he had gone into an exact description of what they did there day by day, year after year, because all his contemporaries knew that anyhow; and if we don't know it any more, it's our own fault. It is only due to lack of interest, to the greatest sin of all, indifference. When we are interested enough, we know how and where to find information on, for instance, how the pharaohs in Egypt lived, just exactly how they embalmed their mummies, and how the aborigines live in Tierra de Fuego. It takes just as much effort to find out about the customs of the Holy Land at the time of Christ. For instance, if we don't know which daily prayers were said in the Holy Family, how the Sabbath was observed, what the school system was like at that time in the Holy Land, what the position of the mother was in the house — well, then we must soberly admit that we are more interested in the pygmies and the old Egyptians than in the daily life of our Lord.

Indifference was the sin which hurt our Lord most, and with which He was most impatient: "I know your works: you are neither cold nor hot. Would that you were cold or hot! So, because you are lukewarm, and neither cold nor hot, I will spew you out of my mouth" (Rev. 3:15–16). If we are not in a position to know for ourselves one complete day in the Holy Family from dawn to dusk, or one week from Sabbath to Sabbath, or one year with the major feasts and pilgrimages to Jerusalem, if we don't know down to details the political situation of our Lord's country and people during His own time, if we don't know the mountains and valleys, the cities and villages and what they looked like, the change of seasons, the flowers and animals — if we don't know this, then we have to admit with a sorry heart that we have sinned gravely through indifference. And there is only one thing to do: Get to work right away.

Very soon the hidden life will not be hidden at all. We see Mary busy in her household from morning till night, starting out early at dawn carrying the day's supply of water from the well into her house in an earthen pitcher on her head. After that we see her grinding the day's portion of meal and baking their daily bread, taking a broom and sweeping the house, preparing the meals, spinning flax and wool, and weaving undergarments, tunics, and mantles, one for the Sabbath and holy days, another one for every day.

And when we learn in detail how these were done — very soon we shall lose this notion that Mary spent her life with eyes raised and hands folded in prayer. She will become a woman of flesh and blood, a mother and housewife; and very soon we shall find ourselves talking things over with her, things which pertain to household and children, the elements of women's talk all over the world. And by "talking things over," we shall have started out on a new life of prayer hitherto unknown to us. We might never use the word "contemplation," but we shall experience the fact that enough meditation automatically leads to quiet contemplation. Not only will Jesus and Mary not be strangers any more, they will really become members of our household, more so perhaps than some of our very own relatives, an uncle or an aunt whom we don't see very often.

Let us start out right away. "They returned into Galilee, to their city, Nazareth." This return may not have been of unmixed joy. Nazareth was a provincial town where everybody knows everybody. Mary and Joseph had left it years ago. Now they came back with the little boy, a few years old. Don't you think all the neighbors would want to know where they had been and what they had been doing all the time?

"In Egypt? No, not really! But why?" Small town gossip was waiting for them.

Then the daily life began with Joseph the father of the house. In the eyes of men it was Joseph, Mary, Jesus, while in the eyes of God it was Jesus, Mary, Joseph. Joseph opened his carpenter shop and began to work for his livelihood. In his workshop he made implements like plows, pieces of furniture such as chests and low tables. He also went out putting roofs of cedar beams on houses. One thing he never, never did — he never made a cross.

This was the most hated gallows which the Romans had brought into the country. While Joseph was busy at this craft, Mary, the "good wife . . . puts her hands to the distaff, and her hands hold the spindle. . . . She looks well to the ways of her household, and does not eat the bread of idleness" (Prov. 31:10–27).

What was Jesus doing when He was seven, eight, nine, ten, years old? He was watching His mother and foster father, and very soon He would imitate them. Soon He would find out that on one day in the week there was a completely different atmosphere around the house. This Holy Day began early the night before. It lasted from sunset to sunset. The workshop would be closed, they would wear their Sabbath clothes, the mother would not cook, but they would eat what she had prepared the day before. The house was especially carefully swept and cleaned.

It was the duty of the mother of every house to light the "Sabbath lamp." Jesus would see His mother do it in her inimitable reverent, loving way, spreading out her hands before the lamp, pronouncing the benediction: "Blessed art Thou, oh Lord our God, King of the universe, who hast sanctified us by Thy commandments and command us to kindle the Sabbath lamp." Then as long as the boy was small, He would see Joseph leave with quick steps and later on return in a markedly different way, slowly and thoughtfully. His mother would explain to Him that the rabbis had pronounced this as the way to go to and from church, as we would say.

The food was what we would call a Sunday dinner. Aren't we interested in finding out what they ate, how it was prepared, and how it was served? If we look at our map, we see Nazareth not very far from the big lake. We know that there were many fishermen. Fish was eaten much more than meat, especially in a small family. A levitical law commanded the eating of a whole animal at once. That is why lambs, kids and calves, eggs, and cheese were preferred to beef. Besides, meat was expensive, and the Holy Family, as we still remember from their behavior in the temple when they couldn't afford the lamb, belonged to what we would call the middle class — not rich and not destitute. They were poor, but not to the extent of misery. Mary and Joseph always made ends meet. But there were no luxuries around.

The workshop must have been a child's paradise for the little boy. What grand toys there were just lying around on the floor!

Then one day He must have begun to accompany His mother to the well. There He heard the women greeting each other with the beautiful word *shalom* (peace). This well still exists. We can show pictures of it to our children.

Jesus was a healthy, normal boy. As such, He would want to play with other boys. The time would come when He would be allowed to go out with them and explore the neighborhood.

And He had to go to school. That was commanded by law. The rabbis even forbade the people to settle in a place where there was no school! School was usually connected with the synagogue in Nazareth. Only the boys went to school, and there they learned to read, but not to write. They were taught two books — the Torah, which is known to us as the Law of the Old Testament, and the Mishnah, a commentary to it, the teachings of the famous rabbis. The little boys sat on the floor in a small circle before their teacher, who would teach them first orally by saying a sentence and having them repeat, repeat, repeat. After they really knew it by heart, then he showed them the script. This was so much the method of the day that the verbs "to teach" and "to learn" were identical with the verb "to repeat." The little ones were not only taught the verses of Holy Scriptures, but they were also taught practical things like behavior, moral conduct, and etiquette. And so, Jesus went to school, like my Johannes and your Tom or Jim. And Mary and Joseph were just as anxious as you and I as to whether He made progress, and He always did.

Luke says, "And the child grew and became strong, filled with wisdom; and the favor of God was upon him." The same Luke who said now the child was "filled of wisdom," would say on the next page that He "increased in wisdom and in stature, and in favor with God and man" (Luke 2:52). Here we come upon something which we cannot explain by mere study of history, geography, or sociology. Here we come across one of the deepest mysteries of our religion, something which is a divine secret and would never have been found out by men if it hadn't been for divine revelation.

You and I can attain to three kinds of knowledge. There is a knowledge we get in a natural way. This is the usual experimental knowledge which we pick up as we grow. Then some people also have infused knowledge. That means knowing, like the prophets, for instance, things which they couldn't possibly have learned in a natural way. And then you and I will one day be capable of still another knowledge when we shall meet God fact to face. And now it is such a marvel to think: from the very first moment of His existence on earth our Lord Jesus Christ enjoyed this vision. He always saw the Father face to face. He also possessed all this intuitive, infused knowledge. Isaiah knew that already when he prophesied about Him: "And the spirit of the LORD shall rest upon him, the spirit of wisdom and understanding, the spirit of counsel and might, the spirit of knowledge and the fear of the LORD" (Isa. 11:2).

Since Jesus possessed it all — always — in these two knowledges He could not grow. And then, oh wonder, He is a little boy like yours and mine, who can grow in wisdom and grace before God and men. This unique mystery can never be explained, it can only be believed. Because Jesus had two natures, a human nature and divine nature in one person, He could advance humanly while He was always in God, with God — while He *was* God. Our theologians call this the Hypostatic Union.

Just what did that mean now in His daily life? Why didn't we begin to ponder about it in our hearts? We shall never be finished, but we have all eternity to continue.

These are the precious years up to His 12th birthday when Jesus was a child. Our children wanted to know whether they observed birthdays and feast days and other anniversaries in the Holy Family. After some thinking we decided that they must have, because Mary and Joseph both understood to the fullest extent what those days really meant in the history of mankind. When the angel asked Mary whether she would agree to be the mother of the Messiah and she answered her immortal, "Behold the handmaid of the Lord," when "the light shone in the darkness" in the cave outside of Bethlehem. They saw these days as days of tremendous grace which the Heavenly Father poured out over His undeserving children. In filial gratitude Mary must always have celebrated the anniversaries, and so in the first Christian families they celebrated just privately among themselves birthdays, holidays, and anniversaries like that of the annunciation, visitation, and presentation.

Let us come back to the thought that Jesus was a real child. Much later He will one day solemnly declare to us how we have to be and what we have to do if we want to go to heaven. He will say it in His straightforward, unsophisticated, unmistakable way when He takes a little boy, points to him and says to the disciples, "Truly, I say to you, unless you be turned and become like children, you will never enter the kingdom of heaven" (Matt. 18:3). Just like that: "If you don't, then you won't." There is absolutely nothing we can do about it, but one day we have to face this phrase and what it means. We get some help in how we have to take it when we think of another incident when our Lord said to him, "Truly, truly, I say to you, unless one is born anew, he cannot see the kingdom of God." Nicodemus, the typical grownup, said, stupefied, "How can a man be born when he is old? Can he enter a second time into his mother's womb and be born?" This brought him a slightly ironical, "Are you a teacher of Israel, and yet you do not understand this?" (John 3:3–10). So when He says: "Unless . . . you become like children," this is parallel, and we are not supposed to ask in the same stupefied way, "How can I become small again after I have grown up?" We know He doesn't mean that. So we face the necessity of having to do research work on the question "What are children?" In what ways do children differ from grownups mentally and spiritually, if the physical comparison is to be disregarded but the word still stands: "Unless you become. . . ." And we are about to make one of the most beautiful discoveries, urged on by the reading of the Gospels.

The most striking difference between little ones and grownups is that little ones cannot worry, because they have no past and no future. They live only in the present moment. Just let us watch children. If they eat, they eat; if they sleep, they sleep. There is a beautiful English word which describes how they do whatever they do. They do everything "wholeheartedly," whereas grownups always are half-hearted. While they do one thing, they have to worry about the past — "Oh, I should never have . . . oh, if only I had." Of the future they contemplate, "My, and what is going to happen when . . . and what will I do or what will I say if. . . ." So they are, in the true sense of the word, split personalities and can never do anything with their whole heart. That's why that grave word is spoken over them. They cannot go to heaven because they cannot fulfill the first and most important commandment, which our Lord said was, "You shall love the Lord your God with all your heart, and with all your soul, and with all your mind" (Matt. 22:37). Only children or childlike souls can do anything with their whole heart. That's the first and most tremendous lesson.

Then we find a few more things. Children are full of confidence. They have not learned yet to be suspicious, and when they stretch out their little arms, what else can you do but take them up?

Children learn by observing and imitating. Before they go to school they have learned a whole language and all the necessary ways of acting and doing in order to go through life: how to eat, how to sleep, etc. They watch the ones they love and trust, father and mother, sisters and brothers. If our Lord wants us to be like little children in this regard, He certainly has supplied the means. He has told us about the Father in heaven, we have the example of His wonderful mother and of all our older sisters and brothers, the generations who have gone before us. We have plenty to watch and imitate. There is just one hitch to it. Even the nicest little boy (or girl as far as that goes) will have his faults. Even the greatest saint will first have had to do an enormous amount of work to become like one of those little ones. But there we have Jesus in the first 12 years of His life when He was also in stature a child, a holy child, the perfect child.

The greatest beauty is now that mentally He will not change — the oneness of purpose, the wholeheartedness with which we see Him do everything, the complete absence of even ability to worry in His character, His watching the Father and imitating Him. How truly He can say, "For I have given you an example, that you also should do as I have done to you" (John 13:15).

In His great understanding of human nature He uses the word "become." "Unless you become as little children. . . ." He knows that the way of the world is this: a little one is hardly out of diapers when he is told approvingly, "Now you are a big boy." When he goes to kindergarten, "Now you are not a baby anymore." When he is in the first grade, "Well, you are not in kindergarten anymore; you are a big boy now." This goes on until in high school he doesn't have to be told that he is a big boy now. He knows it himself. Then one day sooner or later he will be banged on the head by those words of our Lord, and all the growing up will not seem like an achievement any longer, but like something which has to be undone. That is when the "becoming" starts. After we have grown up in the eyes of the world, we have to "grow down" in the eyes of God. We have to. There is no way out if we want to go to heaven. Heaven is full of children; our Lord himself said so. One of the quickest ways to accomplish this "growing down" is to become very much at home in the little house in Nazareth — to watch and to imitate.

In 1938 and 1939 the Trapp family made two trips to the United States following their flight from Austria. Here they are in October 1939. Top row (left to right): Werner and Rupert. Middle row: Father Wasner, Johanna, Maria with baby Johannes, Georg, Hedwig, Martina, and Maria. In front: Agathe, Rosmarie, and Eleonore.

CHAPTER
11

"DID YOU NOT KNOW . . . ?"

Luke says, "Now his parents went to Jerusalem every year at the feast of the Passover. And when he was twelve years old they went up according to custom" (Luke 2:41–42).

We are more or less used to accepting the idea of their taking Him with them to the temple obviously for the first time as we might take our little ones for the first time with us to church. It is very much worthwhile to look at the map and to find out a few things about these pilgrimages, which the Jewish men were obligated to make. There were three major feasts, about which the Book of Deuteronomy says, "Three times a year all your males shall appear before the LORD your God . . . at the feast of unleavened bread, at the feast of weeks, and at the feast of booths. They shall not appear before the LORD empty-handed; every man shall give as he is able" (Deut. 16:16–17).

The greatest of these feasts was the Pasch, the Feast

of Unleavened Bread. The very word "*Pasch*" meant "Pass-over," as this feast was instituted in order to remind the Jews throughout all generations of that unforgettable night when the Angel of Death had passed over the houses of the Isra-elites in Egypt, whose doorposts had been smeared with the blood of a lamb. That is why a lamb had to be offered at the Pasch, and it had to be offered in Jerusalem by the head of every family.

Therefore, when the days of the Pasch came close — it was at the time of the full moon in spring — from all over the world Jews set out towards Jerusalem. The women were not obliged to go along, but the really pious women did, as we know from Hannah, the mother of Samuel, who went every year. Children under 12 years of age were obviously not taken along. There was a twofold coming of age for a Jewish boy. At 12 years he came of age before the law, and at 20 before the state. We in our countries are so used to the number 21 in connection with the coming of age, that we have the feeling 12 is almost too soon. In the Orient, how-ever, girls and boys mature so much earlier that a 12-year-old boy there might be like an 18 year old here.

The Jews living in foreign countries, some many hun-dreds of miles away, were not bound to attend the Pasch every year in Jerusalem, but they wanted to come at least once in their lives. When they had come from such vast dis-tances, they would stay on for those 50 days until the Feast of Weeks, or Pentecost, and after that, return home. Luke tells us about Pentecost: "Now there were dwelling in Jerusa-lem Jews, devout men from every nation under heaven" (Acts 2:5). He continues to enumerate them, and it is very inter-esting to find a map of the world as it was known at the time of Christ and find there "every nation under heaven."

There was a Jewish priest, Josephus Flavius by name, who lived just one generation after our Lord, and who wrote down practically everything of interest about his time. His collected works have been brought out in a giant edition, and although some of it is tedious to read, he is still an almost inexhaustible source of information.[1] He dwells at great length on those feasts and how they were celebrated. He is not always too accurate in numbers they say, and when he comes to talking about himself or his people, he is pretty much conceited, making a kind of wonder child himself. But otherwise we really learn things from him.

If we have made ourselves acquainted with the general picture of the countryside and this month of Nisan, as they called the early spring, we know that the land of Israel would be at its greenest and most beautiful and all the roads leading to Jerusalem would be swarming with pilgrims. Then we pick out that one caravan, the one coming from Nazareth. Pilgrims hardly ever travel alone; merely for safety's sake they prefer to travel in caravans. They also like the companionship, and as they ride on camels or donkeys or walk through the dust of the road, they chant psalms and hymns together and play on their flutes.

In order to go from Galilee to Judea there were two main routes; we can find them on the map. The shortest one would lead through the country of Samaria. Samaria! The people living there were of mixed background, descending partly from the Hebrews and partly from the Gentiles who had been brought in by the kings of the Assyrians. "And the king of Assyria brought people from Babylon, Cuthah, Avva, Hamath, and Sepharvaim, and placed them in the cities of Samaria" (2 Kings 17:24). Because they were of mixed ancestry the Orthodox Jews hated them. To them they were heretics, and there was no worse epithet than to be called "Samaritan." One day the enraged Pharisees would hurl this name at Our Lord: "You are a Samaritan and have a demon" (John 8:48). It sounds almost as if these two things belonged together. The Samaritans were shown this concept in most unmistakable terms.

The rabbis had compiled a whole code of laws and regulations as to how a Jew should behave with a Samaritan. He was allowed to look at him only once, just to make sure he was one. Then he had to avert his eyes and keep them averted. Of course, he was not allowed to touch him or touch anything which had been touched by a Samaritan — and so on and so on. So when we read about all these petty laws, we understand the surprise of the woman at Jacob's well when she says: "How is it that you, a Jew, ask a drink of me, a woman of Samaria?" (John 4:9.) It is really true that whatever we learn of the habits and customs will come in handy later when we lovingly study the public life of our Lord.

The pilgrims from Nazareth had to bring their own provisions for the pilgrimage. Nothing should be bought in Samaria. There were traditional overnight places all mapped out from of old. The first stop used to be made in Engannim. (In Josephus Flavius' work we would find it under the name Ginea, and on a modern map of our days, Jenim.) It is about two miles away from Nazareth, and the first village after the pilgrims were through the plains of Esdraelon. The Samaritans had a temple of their own on Mount Garizim, of which they were very jealous. The Jews constantly rubbed in what they thought of them and their temple, and this didn't make the Samaritans any more friendly towards the Jews. We learn of many hostilities breaking out in more or less bloody ways between them.

After the first night the pilgrims would go into the Samaritan hill country towards Sichem, which lay in a pass between the mountains. There Jacob had given to his people the famous well; and Joseph, the most famous of his sons, was buried there. The second night was spent in famous

Sichem. On the third day they had a 25-mile stretch ahead of them to get to Beeroth. This was already out of the territory of the Samaritans. This was an insignificant little place only 8 miles from Jerusalem, but it will never be forgotten because here it was that a mother discovered she had lost her child. Tradition says that Helena and later the Crusaders built a church in memory of that sorrowful young mother who felt the sword pierce.

Thus, on the last day the pilgrims had only 8 miles more, and would arrive by noon, in plenty of time to find shelter for the night.

All the tombs and sepulchres along the way would be freshly whitewashed so they could be avoided by the pilgrims. Otherwise, if they should stumble over one, they would be liturgically unclean and not be able to celebrate the Pasch. Some day our Lord will feel like calling somebody names, and will say to His adversaries, "You are like whitewashed tombs" (Matt. 23:27), which must be a crushing thing for an Orthodox Jew to be called.

Jesus, who, as a human boy, could add new knowledge and progress in wisdom, was one of the pilgrims in that caravan in this memorable year. We can imagine how He, being of the highest intelligence, asked questions of His mother, with whom He would go to Jerusalem, all along the way, and how He would remember the holy history of His people throughout the ages. When they came into the hill country of Judea, the slopes would be simply covered with flocks of sheep. From Josephus Flavius we learn that once there were more than 120,000 lambs slaughtered in the temple at one Passover. As we know, every lamb had to be eaten by a group of people not less than 10 nor more than 20, so we can figure on an attendance of between two and three millions pilgrims, and we can also figure the size of the flocks of sheep.

We can only guess what the boy Jesus would think when He saw all those happy young lambs skipping about in the pastures. Even the infused knowledge He had was much greater than that of all prophets and all angels together, so He must have known also in a human way what would happen to "the Lamb of God" 21 years hence.

On the next morning the pilgrims would catch their first glimpse of Jerusalem, the Holy City, and there, glittering, with its golden roof, the temple — the temple! *Beth jahweh*, it was called — the House of God. What must the boy Jesus have felt when He saw the House of His Father for the first time. The Holy Family went into the Holy City by the northern gate.

The holy writers would remark on the handsomeness of young David and the wisdom of young Solomon. Here was more than David, here was more than Solomon — but no one seemed to notice a thing and, unrecognized, the Lord of heaven and earth came unto His own city and again, His own knew Him not.

Joseph would get busy procuring the paschal lamb, and, knowing boys, it is more than likely that Jesus accompanied him. They had to find out also with whom they would join up to make a company of ten, to buy the bitter herbs and all that was needed for the celebration of the feast. All this had to be done before the end of the afternoon on the day before the feast.

When thinking back on the many folk customs we had in Austria, and how one responds as a child, with eagerness and expectations at certain traditions being repeated in a certain way, it is most striking. This young boy not only watched the preparations for the observance of the holy customs, He knew that it all was merely a symbol and He would be the fulfillment. With what eagerness did He watch!

And now we see them celebrate the feast. Every part

of the ancient ceremony is described, the prayers which were uttered by Jesus, Mary, and Joseph are written down. All we have to do is look for it and tarry a little to add out of our own hearts the emotions, which may have gone through those holiest of hearts. After all, their beloved Jesus would now be a Son of the law, no child any more. That is what singled out this Pasch from the others.

The Jews were not obliged to stay in Jerusalem for all the seven days of the Passover, but the really zealous ones did. Therefore, it must be the old Holy Week which Luke means when he says: "And when the feast was ended, as they were returning, the boy Jesus stayed behind in Jerusalem. His parents did not know it" (Luke 2:43). When the pilgrims from Nazareth assembled at the northern gate, which was called the Damascus Gate, Jesus was not among them. Mary must have thought, *Now as He is of age, He will be with Joseph and the men.* Joseph might have thought, *He doesn't want to let His mother travel alone amid strangers; He must be with her.*

It must have been a most picturesque sight at this Damascus Gate because all the traffic going north, all the Galileans and the strangers from Trachonitis and Abilene, Damascus, and as far as Antioch would organize into caravans there. As they left the gate they would sing one of the psalms of the Hallel. Again, it is worth pondering about what Mary and Joseph may have been thinking about — and what had happened to Jesus? He may not have known until the very morning of this day when He was ready to join His caravan that the will of the Father was otherwise. As we shall see later, the will of the Father was everything and all. "For I have come down from heaven, not to do my own will, but the will of him who sent me" (John 6:38).

This is now a great mystery, why the Father retained the Son in the temple. Did He want to give Him three days of vacation, so to speak, and allow Him to dwell in His presence as a human being in the closest way possible in those days, in the temple? We don't know. We can only ponder and wonder. We can want to know. We can ask the Holy Ghost, who, as our Lord promised, would some day explain everything to us. Everything — what a word! Until that day we just have to assume that the Father wished Jesus to stay in the temple, and Jesus stayed without notifying Mary and Joseph. This adds to the mystery. Why bring all this anxiety on those good people, who had done nothing all these years but try to be the best possible keepers of the treasure entrusted to their care? Until the Holy Ghost explains this better to us, we just have to take what is written in Holy Scriptures: "For my thoughts are not your thoughts, neither are your ways my ways, says the LORD" (Isa. 55:8).

Then came that crucial evening when the caravan would stop over again in Beeroth. That was arranged on purpose. In case somebody had forgotten something or somebody was left behind, it would not be too hard to catch up with the caravan. And now comes the moment when Mary, who hadn't seen her boy for a full day, eagerly went over to find Joseph and her child. Joseph, on the other hand, was as eager to see his family and be reunited with them for the evening meal as was customary in those caravans where the men and women traveled separately. Seeing each other, *the one question* they must have asked simultaneously and most anxiously was, "Where is Jesus?" And the horrified answer, "I don't know. I thought He was with you." What a terrible moment! The very next thing to do would be to look all over the caravan, but nobody had seen Him. Nobody knew. The only conclusion therefore was that He must have been left behind in Jerusalem. They would turn around immediately and go back.

Some books suggest that on the first day Mary and

Joseph traveled as far as the overnight stop and on the second day they traveled back to Jerusalem. I don't think so. How could they have closed an eye? How could they have waited an unnecessary minute?

Years ago we were traveling in our big bus on a concert tour somewhere in New Hampshire, heading north. Some time in the afternoon I turned around from my seat and said, "Lorli, tell me, have you . . . " and then I noticed that the seat where Lorli always sat was empty. I turned all the way around and got up and looked, and sure enough, she was not in the bus. Now eager talking and guessing started. The driver stopped. We had been driving for quite a number of hours with no rest. The last stop had been somewhere in Massachusetts, on the highway, to get a map of New Hampshire.

Lorli was then a young child, maybe about as old as Jesus when He stayed behind in the temple. She must have slipped out unnoticed when we stopped at that gas station and now — where was she and what had happened to her meanwhile? All the stories of kidnapping and gangsters stood out in my mind and imagination can turn into your worst enemy at such times. Of course, we called the police, but the State Police of New Hampshire couldn't do anything in Massachusetts, and we had to go back all the way. Finally we found her at the police headquarters listening in rapt attention to the stories of some of the highway patrolmen.

Just from this little anecdote I know Mary and Joseph would turn around immediately. It was the time around full moon and the road would be light enough. This way back would be an ordeal when we think of all the caravans emerging towards the north, and Mary and Joseph worming their way through them. One very anxious thought must have troubled them most, the same thought which bothered us so much when we had turned around in the bus. Perhaps Lorli had gotten a ride in some car and we might miss her on the highway. So what if Jesus were amid the crowd constantly passing in the other direction? Finally they came to Jerusalem, having traveled 16 miles, maybe not having eaten and probably near collapse.

The first place to go would be to their last night's lodgings. We don't know, however, whether they stayed with acquaintances or whether they camped in one of those innumerable white tents which were scattered all over the countryside outside the walls of Jerusalem. Then I am sure Mary and Joseph went straight to the temple. At this point it will really come in handy that we have spent so much time on the temple previously, so that we know about those huge halls and stairways and galleries and cloisters, and we know that at this time about 200,000 people were milling around with all the noise of the Orient. Of course, they would ask the different members of the temple police whether they had seen their boy. Oh — they had seen so many boys, but they didn't remember *the* boy.

Now they must have gone out searching through the narrow streets for a whole day and a whole night, both weary to exhaustion. Joseph may have remembered another time when he saw Mary "drooping with fatigue"; and Mary felt the sword turning in her heart mercilessly. She hadn't had any warning. Never, never had Jesus caused them any anxiety or any trouble. Out of the blue sky had this cruel surprise come; and — was this the end? Would she never see Him again? Had He vanished out of their lives? Had He been kidnapped by some who had perhaps found out His identity or had He been kidnapped and sold as a slave like Joseph of old? Nothing had been revealed to her. She was not prepared, so her imagination must have run wild as that of every anxious mother in such a situation does. Where was He? What had happened to Him?

On the Sabbath and especially on high feasts the members of the Sanhedrin had established a custom of scattering throughout the temple and giving instructions on the Scriptures to the people. They would seat themselves on a stool, the people at their feet. They would take a text of the Holy Books and start explaining it. After they had finished, there would always be a discussion. The people would eagerly ask questions and listen attentively to the answers, wisdom dropping from the lips of their venerated elders.

In those days the rabbis may have singled out a special boy by the very questions He asked. They must have been delighted by the understanding this youngster showed and by the beautiful manners He displayed, the modesty, humility, courtesy, and, in addition, the highest intelligence they had ever found among their own pupils. At the end of the first and second days the rabbis, after having spent their time with the people, may have commented among themselves on this boy; and on the third day they came together in a group enjoying the boy. "After three days, they found him in the temple, sitting among the teachers, listening to them and asking them questions; and all who heard him were amazed at his understanding and his answers" (Luke 2:46–47).

Again and again Mary and Joseph must have tried the temple, but the hour had not yet come, as it will be said several times in His life later. He must have been concealed from their eyes in the throng and they did not see Him. One the third day, however, the Holy Ghost led their steps over to where Jesus was sitting in the midst of the teachers of Israel. When they saw Him so calm and so matter-of-course, the first thought they had must have been, *He has not been lost. He must have stayed behind knowing what He did.* "And when they saw him they were astonished." This we can well imagine. Never had they seen Him like this before: this new light in His eyes and a new dignity surrounding Him, which was somehow mirrored in the faces of the venerable old teachers, who treated Him almost as an equal. Mary and Joseph waited until they had finished and then His mother said to Him: "Son, why have you treated us so? Behold, your father and I have been looking for you anxiously" (Luke 2:48).

Here we see Mary in a very special light. Later in His life it would happen that when our Lord's best friends got an inkling of who He really was, they would somehow withdraw in awe and refuse to let Him humble himself. So we see John the Baptist exclaim, "I need to be baptized by you, and do you come to me?" (Matt. 3:14). And when our Lord was about to kneel down before Peter in order to wash his feet, Peter would refuse most excitedly, "You shall never wash my feet" (John 13:8). And the Baptist and Peter had at that time only a fair idea of who Jesus really was.

Mary, however, knew it all the time. Humanly speaking, she must have felt from the very beginning like saying, "My Lord and My God, how could I ever act as authority over You? You must command me, not I You." It is always attributed to the humility of John and Peter that they acted the way they did; but we have to say that Mary's humility far outreached theirs. All these years she was obligated to accept services from her child, who also was her God, and to instruct Him and command Him. Now we see her ask Him a question which sounds almost like a reproach. Every well-brought-up Jewish boy, upon hearing this, would get up and apologize humbly. Jesus did not, but answered, "How is it that you sought me? Did you not know that I must be in my Father's house?" (Luke 2:49).

Of all the things which happened in those heart-rending days, the words, "Did you not know?" must have been the worst, because they somehow implied that they should have known or could have known. Well — all we can say is, if Jesus himself could grow in wisdom and grace before God and men, He who was God at the same time, how much more is this true of Mary and Joseph who, after all, were only human. Both of them knew the secret mystery of this child, but still they did not quite understand the word that He spoke to them. This must have been the first manifestation of His being the Son of the Heavenly Father. With great tact, Jesus at first does not contradict when Mary says "Behold, your father and I have been looking for you anxiously," but then He immediately refers to God as His Father, the only one He would accept.

As He was the child in the family, Mary had a certain natural claim on Jesus — and Jesus does not deny it. Very soon He will prove how highly He regards that, but right now He has to inform them about His heavenly vocation. On a later day He will say, "He who loves father or mother more than me is not worthy of me; and he who loves son or daughter more than me is not worthy of me" (Matt. 10:37). "Truly, I say to you, there is no one who has left house or brothers or sisters or mother or father or children or lands, for my sake and for the gospel, who will not receive a hundredfold now in this time; houses and brothers and sisters and mothers and children and lands, with persecutions, and in the age to come eternal life" (Luke 2:49).

These were the first words spoken by Jesus as the Son of God and the Son of Man, which were written down in the Gospels. They seem almost like the title to His life story, because in His entire life He will do nothing else but be about His Father's business.

More than 1,900 years have passed since, and nobody has fully grasped the depths of these words, "Did you not know . . . ?" Luke informs us that Mary and Joseph "did not understand the saying which he spoke to them. . . . and his mother kept all these things in her heart" (Luke 2:50–51). A life full of pondering and contemplating on these and all His words will make Mary advance and grow to such an extent that never again will He have to say, "Did you not know . . . ?"

CHAPTER
12

THE CARPENTER

I n the good old times when the craftsmen were the back
bone of every country, and every village and every small
town had its own blacksmith, tailor, shoemaker, tanner
and, of course, carpenter, young boys between 12 and 14
would be taken on as apprentices. They had to learn the
craft from scratch. When an apprentice had learned how to
handle all the tools and he did not spoil anything any more,
he advanced to the next stage, journeyman. That meant that
he was working side by side with the master for a number
of years until he was good enough to start his own workshop. Then he had to make his masterpiece, with which he
showed all his skill.

Unfortunately, these things are dying out so fast that
our children will only know about them through books. This
is the beginning of the end for every country. Coming from
a country in Europe where the crafts are still at their height
and good craftsmen greatly esteemed, we all missed them

very much when we came to America. The first years in New York and Philadelphia were not so bad. We were used to the fact that in the elegant Kaerntnerstrasse in Vienna you didn't see craft shops with the master working in the window either, but when we moved up to northern New England, that's when we started worrying. We found out that the blacksmith in Stowe, who was a great artist in his craft, just couldn't find an apprentice. The same thing has happened to Mr. Stafford, the wonderful tinsmith, to Ben our town cobbler, and that's about all the crafts we have left. The young boys of this generation are not interested in learning a craft. Sometimes you find a rich boy who takes up a craft for a hobby; but that's not the right thing. He doesn't have to live from his handiwork, so he will not put his whole heart into it.

When the Son of God became a man, what did He choose to be? A carpenter. Not as a hobby, but to make a living.

At first He was apprenticed to Joseph, the carpenter. He started out by learning to use the tools, by doing little easy jobs, but mostly by watching the master. At 16 or 17 He was already working steadily with His foster father, being at least as good as he, if not better; because we can be sure that the Son-of-God-made-man was not only of high intelligence, filled with the greatest wisdom of mind and soul, but He also had the most skillful hands.

"And he went down with them and came to Nazareth, and was obedient to them. . . . And Jesus increased in wisdom and in stature, and in favor with God and man" (Luke 2:51–52). We are now setting out to explore the famous "hidden life," which already is much less hidden to us because we know so much about His first 12 years. We see them get up at sunrise and go to sleep at sunset, a practice absolutely unknown to modern man. But oil and candles were expensive, and theirs was a life of frugality. We see the two men working either in the work shop or somewhere on a building according to the words of Genesis 3:19: "In the sweat of your face you shall eat bread." Paul will later declare firmly: "If any one will not work, let him not eat" (2 Thess. 3:10). The Holy Family submitted fully to this plan of God. We see the woman of the house working all day long to do all her housework, heavy and light. She also had her craft, spinning and weaving.

We see Jesus grow up and when we want to find out what He did in those long 18 years in Nazareth, we finally see that He prayed, He obeyed, and He worked; and not only He alone, but all three of them.

They prayed; we can find their daily prayers, we can find out how they observed the Day of the Lord. They must have recited the hymns, prayers, and psalms contained in Holy Scriptures, and during many hours of their working day their thought dwelt on the hidden meaning of what their lips had recited. That's what they did when they were pondering.

They obeyed: "And Mary said, "Behold, I am the handmaid of the Lord; let it be to me according to your word" (Luke 1:38), and: "Did you not know that I must be in my Father's house?" (Luke 2:49). These words uttered by Mary and Jesus give a deep insight into their life of constant obedience to the Father. From Joseph we know how promptly he reacted each time an angel came. Theirs was a family life of obedience to the will of God.

Books and books and books have been written on family life. Our magazines and newspapers are full of alarming articles on the danger of family life crumbling in our days. Psychiatrists, psychoanalysts, and psychologists are busy in research to answer the question "why." Little do they seem to know that this question was answered two thousand years ago by a few words in the Gospel of Luke. There we see the Heavenly Father making this tremendous new foundation, the Christian family, when He sends His Son to the small home in Nazareth. It is absolutely impossible to meditate too much on the hidden life. Just watching Jesus, Mary, and Joseph in their daily routine will do something for us. There is our model, and there is our only remedy. As the saying from the old country has it: If there are more mothers like Mary and more fathers like Joseph, there will be more children like Jesus.

CHAPTER
13

THE SON OF MAN

When later Jesus would come to the synagogue in Nazareth in order to preach there, the people would ask, "Is not this the carpenter, the son of Mary?" (Mark 6:3) A son would only be spoken of in this way if the father were dead. Another time some relatives of Jesus wanted to bring Him home. They would never have interfered if the father of the house had been living. And when our Lord gave His mother into the care of John, His disciple, then it is definitely sure that Joseph, her husband, was dead. Through tradition we learn that Joseph died when Jesus was 18 years old. If this is really true, then Jesus and Mary must have gotten a legal guardian, usually one of the relatives, to take care of their affairs until the Son would be 20 years old.

There have always been references to the happiness of Joseph's death because he died in the presence of Jesus and Mary. When we think that Jesus would later break out in

123

tears and cry at His friend's tomb — how much more would He have shown His grief when His foster father died, he who was so much nearer and dearer to Him than Lazarus. When the dying Joseph saw the tears in the eyes of his Lord and God and understood that they were shed for him — we can understand that his was a happy death.

Now it was even more quiet in the little house where a widow maintained her family. When Jesus was 20 years old, He became of age before the state. He took over officially the responsibility and care of His mother, and He was now the heir to all of Joseph's possessions. From now on He was the Master of the house. Until then He had been "subject to them." From now on when a question was to be decided, Mary would bring it to Jesus and He would decide.

Many mysteries are contained in these next ten years when Jesus and Mary lived so close together. Outwardly we can reconstruct to a great extent their simple and uncomplicated life, but how must it have been in their souls?

To understand even the lightest little bit about Mary, we shall have to go back to paradise when God had created men according to His image and likeness. We would have to meditate at length on what Adam and Eve were like before the Fall. How much do we know about how life was in the state of grace, when men could converse with God like children with their Father, when they used to walk with Him in the garden every day in the evening breeze?

There is a great deal to be found out by meditating on mankind before and after sin. It is exasperating how little we know of things which we could know, only because we don't think about them. The worst part of our ignorance is that we don't even know how ignorant we are.

It must have been a mystery to Mary that her Son, whom she knew to be the Messiah, went right on as a carpenter even when He was 25, 28, or 29 years old. But in her state of grace she knew no curiosity. She may not even have asked Him what He planned to do.

How must it have been for Him? As man on His early pilgrimages to Jerusalem He saw His Father's house made into a den of thieves. He was just as outraged about it in His innermost soul when He was 25 or 29 as a little later when He would take a little scourge or ropes. There we learn something of His long-suffering patience in waiting for His hour to come.

Maria von Trapp — storyteller, singer, and spokesperson
for the Trapp Family Choir.

A WORD IN BETWEEN

Usually books have only forewords or introductions. I have come to a spot in this book now where I want very badly to explain something about what is to come. First I had it in the foreword, which I shrewdly called "how it happened," just in case there are other people like me who always skip forewords. But it didn't really fit in that place. I couldn't possibly say it in the text either, so please allow me to say "a word in between."

This book really does not want to become a "life of Christ." It only wants to serve as a stimulus to all families to reconstruct their own "life of Christ," parents and children together, simply by telling what we did. One of the reasons why it is so wonderful to search through the life of Christ as a family is that children always ask questions and expect answers, honest answers. And if you say, "I really don't know," they will ask, "Couldn't you find out?"

After having finished reading *Yesterday, Today, and Forever*, you might have one big question on your mind: "But where in the world did you find all this information, all these many details of the childhood story of our Lord, which only takes a few pages in my New Testament?"

There I must answer: aren't we lucky — and by "we" I mean all people of our days. A generation or two ago all the precious knowledge about the circumstances of the land

and times of Christ politically, socially, and spiritually, as well as the findings of archaeologists, were hidden away in great scholarly works, some of them written in Latin, Greek, or Hebrew. They were locked up in professional libraries, inaccessible to the common man. Within our own generation, however, there have appeared on the market a number of most helpful books. Scholars have dedicated a whole lifetime to compiling this information and giving it to us in readable English. There are Gospel commentaries like *Jesus Christ* by Leonce de Grandmaison; *The Gospel of Jesus Christ* by Marie Joseph LaGrange; *The Public Life of Our Lord Jesus Christ* by Archbishop Alban Goodier; *The Life of Our Lord Jesus Christ* by Maurice Meschler; *Life of Jesus* by Francois Mauriac; *The Life of Christ* by Guiseppe Ricciotti; *Jesus Christ: His Life, His Teaching, and His Work* by Ferdinand Prat; *Mary the Mother of Jesus* by Franz M. William; then the two precious books by Father Denis O'Shea, *Mary and Joseph, Their Life and Times* and *The Holy Family.*[1]

Every home should also have a Bible encyclopedia in one volume with many illustrations. There you can look up anything you want to know about agriculture, flowers, herbs, trees, animals, wearing apparel, arts and crafts, business transactions, villages, towns, cities, homes, nutrition, and worship.

In the summer we conduct a camp. It is a music camp, and it lies at the foot of the hill where we live. There we conduct four "Sing Weeks" every year, each of which is ten days long. The third one is always a Liturgical Sing Week, dealing with church music and questions of the liturgy, and for this Sing Week there are usually quite a number of priests, seminarians, and sisters. A number of wonderful friendships have been formed through the camp, and these friends return to us whenever they can come, even if the camp is not open. Then they come to our house, and there in the living room is the famous bay window, famous for the most interesting and wonderful discussions we have had there with them. The remarkable thing has happened, and still does: whatever the problem under discussion may be, it will invariably lead to taking our copies of the New Testament and searching through its pages for the answer which, of this we are dead sure, it must contain.

By the way, this word, "problem," has only slipped in here. It should really be eliminated from the vocabulary of a Christian. When we look at the first Christian era, we see there were no problems. If something came their way in the line of adversities, they treated it first as an obstacle. An obstacle we have to overcome. We have to do everything in our power to get rid of it. Only after we have tried everything and it still doesn't move, then we know. This is not an obstacle, this is a cross. If obstacles are meant to be overcome, crosses are meant to be borne, and, if we can manage at all, borne gladly according to His example. "Problems" are a dangerous hybrid of modern times. They seem to be meant only and solely to be talked about. How often you find when you earnestly try to help somebody with his problems, you learn to your own astonishment that he doesn't really want that. He needs problems in order to be able to talk about himself.

This is a disease of our time. Just watch little children — they never have problems. They may have obstacles to encounter, and no one is as persistent as a little child trying to overcome an obstacle! They may have, small as they are, a cross to carry, and it is very touching to watch how patiently children suffer. But in their life is no room for a problem. They are not yet busy with themselves. Then we have our Lord. He most certainly had obstacles to overcome, and He did it with flying colors. When it was the time to fight, whether it was the Pharisees or at times His own slow-witted disciples or His own tiredness, or Satan with all his pomp and all his works, He showed us how to fight obstacles. And when the time came when the Father sent Him the cross, He most certainly showed what to do with a cross. But in His whole life there was no problem. We shall be astonished when we notice how often that word creeps into our conversation, but we should consciously fight it.

We in the family have done it now quite often, starting at the beginning and going with Him through His life as much as possible day by day, 365 days a year for those first 30 years, most of them spent in Nazareth; and then watching how He leaves His peaceful home because the Father is calling. His time is fulfilled — His hour has come. Now come the last thousand days of His life. After we have watched Him and listened to Him in the most varied situations, one thought finally sticks in our minds, when He says at the end: "For I have given you an example, that you also should do as I have done to you" (John 13:15). From then on only one thing matters in our life: to find out what Jesus would do, how He would react, what He would say in our stead as we go from day to day.

While sitting in the bay window, usually having a cup of coffee right after lunch or right after supper, all kinds of difficulties will come up for discussion. Very often a startled, perplexed silence will follow when we are confronted with the question: what would our Lord do in such a case? The thing to do then is for everyone to take his own copy of the New Testament and, sitting around the octagonal table with the coffee, one has to thumb through the pages and look for something which fits the situation. Isn't it glorious and almost incredible that we have never looked in vain?

This frequent thumbing through the Gospels — besides bringing the answers to our questions — has another wonderful effect, and a twofold one. Not only do we really find our way around the Gospels very soon and know that this comes only in Luke, whereas that only John talks about, and something else can only be found in Matthew or Mark; but we also learn to know Him better and better. Now it is not so much His times and their customs that we are getting to know; now it is His own character. More and more we are overwhelmed by what we find. It is heartwarming.

A stop for a concert in San Francisco, 1946.

PART TWO

TODAY

CHAPTER
14

THE OTHER CHEEK

I t was pouring outside. The Worcestor Range beyond Stowe Hollow couldn't even be seen, it was so foggy. Such weather invites one to prolong one of those coffee sessions. In the bay window were four priests, a few seminarians, and some of us. Maria was "boring." This is a family joke which goes back to our first year in America. After a concert we were invited to a reception in somebody's house, and obviously as a special lure to us, it was said that Mrs. So-and-So was pouring. Our Martina, very young then and always known for her rather careless diction, said to our aghast hostess, "What does it mean that Mrs. So-and-So is boring?"

It traveled fast from lady to lady and was the joke of the evening because it so happened, the hostess told us under her breath, that Mrs. So-and-So *was* boring!

That has stuck with us ever since, and whenever the coffee pot is brought in, somebody raises the question, "And who is boring today?"

"I have such difficulties with 'the other cheek,' " began Father O'Shaughnessy. "I just can't understand it. It doesn't seem right to me. It doesn't seem manly. If someone strikes me on the right cheek, does it mean that I should really and truly turn the other one also? Or if someone steals my coat, that I should run after him and offer him my suit also? I just don't get it."

"Doesn't that serve as an introduction to 'But I say to you, love your enemies'?" asked Father Di Silva.

"Let's get our New Testaments," I suggested. That was a nice little break. Everyone had to get up to get his copy, and meanwhile we could do a little thinking. Sure, there we found it:

> You have heard that it was said, "An eye for an eye and a tooth for a tooth." But I say to you, Do not resist one who is evil. But if any one strikes you on the right cheek, turn to him the other also; and if any one would sue you and take your coat, let him have your cloak as well; And if any one forces you to go one mile, go with him two miles. Give to him who begs from you, and do not refuse him who would borrow from you.
>
> You have heard that it was said, "You shall love your neighbor and hate your enemy." But I say to you, Love your enemies and pray for those who persecute you, so that you may be sons of your Father who is in heaven; for he makes his sun rise on the evil and one the good, and sends rain on the just and on the unjust. For if you love those who love you, what reward have you? Do not even the tax collectors do the same? And if you salute only your brethren, what more are you doing than others? Do not even the Gentiles do

the same? You, therefore, must be perfect, as your heavenly Father is perfect (Matt. 5:38–48).

"Before we get into any arguments, let's look now at what our Lord himself did with these words in His own life," began our Father Wasner. "Let's turn the pages and stop wherever we find something under the heading: our Lord and His enemies."

We started reading, and whoever found something, read it aloud. One of us had paper and pencil to write down the place and something like a resume of the quotation. In about two hours we had gone through the four Gospels and had found about 90 places where our Lord was either dealing with His enemies or discussing the subject with His disciples. Now we took those different passages, read them, tried to compare them, and all of a sudden something occurred to us. Whenever our Lord met enemies who were His very own personal enemies, He always reacted with meekness and humility, and with so much patience.

For instance, the first enemy in His life was Herod, who wanted to destroy Him. Meekly and humbly He fled from him. We always have to keep in mind that His was not the case of the ordinary refugee who hasn't much choice but to flee. At any moment our Lord would have defended himself, as He said so unmistakably to His disciples in Gethsemane: "Do you think that I cannot appeal to my Father, and he will at once send me more than twelve legions of angels?" (Matt 26:53.) If we keep this always in our mind — what He could have done to His enemies — only then are we duly impressed in watching what He actually did. Any number of times the scribes or Pharisees wanted to catch Him with a tricky question. He knew that. For the longest time, instead of giving way to His righteous indignation, He would tolerate them, answering their questions quietly but with divine thoroughness as if pleading with them, "Don't you see how wrong you are?"

After a few years of this method, the disciples seem to have had enough of it, seeing that the adversaries were only getting fresher and didn't seem to be converted through His patience. They wanted to show the Pharisees their place by force. Take the time when He wanted to enter a Samaritan town and the Samaritans did not allow Him. When James and John the Apostles saw this, they were outraged. "Lord," they cried, "wilt thou that we command fire to come down from heaven, and consume them, even as Elias did?" But no, that was not what He wanted. "Ye know not what manner of spirit ye are of. For the Son of man is not come to destroy men's lives, but to save them" (Luke 9:54-56;KJV).

We see Him go fearlessly through His last days, uncompromising with His enemies, but always with an outstretched hand. He could not have shown this in a more touching way than when the traitor finally caught Him in the garden and Jesus said imploringly, "Friend, why are you here?" (Matt. 26:50) Just a few short hours ago He had warned this man. This is now the fullness of "turning the other cheek" when He says to Judas, "Friend." On the cross He will sum up His whole attitude towards His personal enemies, His willingness to forgive and forget: "Father, forgive them; for they know not what they do" (Luke 23:34). "If any one would sue you and take your coat, let him have your cloak as well" (Matt. 5:40), He had said before. Now on the cross they have not only taken His coat, they have taken all, so they think, even His life. And after His death He will give still a little more than they have taken. A lance will open His Heart, and the last drop of His blood He will give. In such greatness do we see Him live His own words.

But then there is another element in meeting if they are not His own private, personal antagonists, if they happen to be enemies of the Father, doing wrong towards Him who has sent our Lord. Then we see Him very differently. "And making a whip of cords, he drove them all . . . out of the temple. . . . Take these things away; you shall not make my Father's house a house of trade" (John 2:15–16). He shouts at them. When the Pharisees and scribes have had sufficient time, when He has pleaded long enough with them, showing them by miracles that He really is "the One," and when there is no more doubt that they simply don't want to believe, then they turn from being His private enemies into being the enemies of God. They have rejected His divine grace, and they are responsible that others might miss it, too. There we see our Lord in anger and wrath. One can almost see His lips tremble and hear His voice shout when He addressed them: "You blind guides, straining out a gnat and swallowing a camel! . . . Woe to you scribes and Pharisees, hypocrites! for you are like whitewashed tombs, which outwardly appear beautiful, but within they are full of dead men's bones and all uncleanness. . . . You serpents, you brood of vipers, how are you to escape being sentenced to hell?" (Matt. 23:24–33).

"That brings home a point to me," said Father Jackson, a wonderful elderly priest, "and it gets stronger by the minute as I look at these verses. Don't we usually react in just the opposite way to our Lord's way? When anyone shows up as His personal enemy, He is meek and humble and practically takes the person on His lap; but when it comes to the honor of God, then He speaks His mind fearlessly, and never mind what might happen to Him afterwards. And we? How often does it happen that in our company things are said which are definitely against God or His Church or His commandments, and if we can manage at all, we turn a deaf ear so as not to get into an embarrassing situation; but woe if anyone steps on our own toes! Then we are up in arms. Am I right?"

At this moment the bell rang. What could that mean? I was stupefied myself, because the bell usually rings only for meals. But — looking at my watch, I saw it right there and then. It has happened before that while we were engaged in such conversations, the hours have passed like minutes.

As the dinner bell had interrupted us in the middle of a sentence, the conversation went right on during supper. And when we sat once more around the coffee in the bay window afterwards, Father O'Shaughnessy asked the momentous question, "But just how does one do it? I do understand now what 'turning the other cheek' really means, but in practical everyday life — how do I love my enemy?"

Between three of us — each one sounded as if he would know what he was talking about — we tried to answer this question.

You may very well have lived a long life, saying the Lord's Prayer daily, and when you came to the words "and forgive us our trespasses as we forgive those who trespass against us," your soul was completely quiet and unruffled. Then one day something happens. It may all be your own fault. You may have a bad argument and the other one walks out on you, bitter and full of wrath. Before you can think twice, you have an enemy. At first, you don't want to believe it. You say to yourself, he'll come around, just wait a little. But this happens to be one of those unfortunate cases where he does not come around. After awhile you may say that it is perfectly ridiculous, and you may earnestly try to meet him, and in a casual way get things straightened out. But then you find out that he's fed up with you and he has no intention whatsoever of having things as they were. Soon you will hear how he spoke about you on this or that occasion, and from those remarks you know now that you have an enemy.

Soon after this startling discovery, these words emerge from the depths of your memory and they take on a completely new meaning: "You have heard that it was said, 'You shall love your neighbor and hate your enemy.' But I say to you, Love your enemies and pray for those who persecute you" (Matt. 5:43–44).

And now, a new period in your life begins. You try, you really try, to love your enemy — but how? There have been a number of different loves in your life and these you try to apply now to him. How you loved your parents when you were very young yourself — how you loved your best friend in school — how you loved in those unique weeks before your wedding — how you now love your own children. Then there is in your heart love for your country, for your hometown, for your old school, and your neighborhood. It is perfectly amazing how many shades of love move a human heart during one short life. But, as hard as you may try, not one of them fits your purpose. Now, you almost get worried because there is that command: "But I say to you . . ." and you haven't yet found a way to fulfill it. This much you have learned, however, that the love for your enemy is a completely new love in your life and you have to discover it step by step.

All you are doing now is wanting to love your enemy. As you want to love him, you are getting very much concerned about him, and this is the first step. You realize that he really shouldn't be your enemy — nobody really should stubbornly resist reconciliation — and with an anxious heart you realize that it cannot do him much good.

As the natural outcome of this, your concern, you find yourself talking with God about your enemy. This is the second step. You say: "Dear Lord, please don't take this too seriously; I really don't think he means it quite the way it sounds. Don't forget how much I antagonized him, and please, dear Lord, I want you to know there is not bitterness in my heart against him whatever he might say or do." There's a great urge in your heart to make sure about this because you realize that if you get angry and bitter and have your own spiritual life badly influenced by all this, it would be partly his fault and he would be held responsible.

As time goes on, you discover that there is a change taking place in yourself. Since that person of whom you thought so highly, who was so close to you and to whom you were so much attached has turned against you, you find that you get more and more detached from other people, because you are aware that what happened once could happen any day again. And there you find that your enemy has done you a great service, and most eagerly you point that out in your next talks with God. This is the third step. However, even if it has helped you, it should not continue. You would not want to die or want him to die, still your enemy. Now you begin to storm heaven. "The return of the brother" becomes your foremost intention. You ask all your friends to help you pray for a "certain intention." And whatever comes your way in the line of suffering is greeted with a smile, be it physical pain or mental anguish, because it can be used to be offered up for the most important person in your life, your enemy. This is the last step.

Now you have found the love for your enemy. It is completely different from all other loves, and it is very anxious and very unemotional. It resides mostly in your will, but let us hope that in the eyes of God it is a soaring fire which, in His own good time, will melt all the ice or resistance. And our Lord's wish will be fulfilled: "That they may be one . . . that they may become perfectly one" (John 17:22–23).

CHAPTER
15

"I Have Called You Friends"

The next day was one of those beautiful days which make every visitor exclaim at the view from our mountaintop. They have never seen anything like it. We wanted to make up to our friends who had been sitting indoors for quite some time, and we took them across the valley to the opposite mountain range up to the Stowe Pinnacle. After a stiff climb of about two hours we emerged from the woods onto that huge rock which crowns the Pinnacle like a cupola. There we feasted our eyes on a 360-degree view. Then we had a picnic lunch.

Father Jones said, "I could hardly get to sleep last night. I kept thinking about our discussion. I wonder, could we do it once more and find out something about Our Lord and His friends?"

"I don't think right now, Father," I said, "because we would need our New Testaments."

Lo and behold, out of coat pockets, vest pockets, and

knapsacks appeared little books. Everybody had brought his New Testament — except me. Was this a conspiracy? No — everybody had just "hoped we would do it again."

"I can truthfully say," said Father Jackson, pipe dangling, "that I have read and meditated a great deal on the Scriptures in my life, but it never felt as good as yesterday with all of us working on one topic. Light just seemed to stream out of the lines. Did anyone else feel like that?"

Looking around, he met only with eager nods. I knew so well what he meant, from our family sessions. After all, our Lord had once said, "For where two or three are gathered in my name, there am I in the midst of them" (Matt. 18:20). In earlier years when the children were small, we used to have an empty chair for our Lord, who had promised to be in our midst. This is an altogether different presence from the omnipresence of God. It is a very real presence, however, and one can always feel something of the sensation of the two disciples walking to Emmaus as they expressed it afterwards: "Did not our hearts burn within us while he talked to us on the road, while he opened to us the scriptures?" (Luke 24:32).

We sat in a circle, and someone remarked, "This is almost as good as in the bay window."

"Except for the coffee," said Father Jackson swinging his pipe.

Soon we were deeply involved in turning pages, watching Jesus with His friends. All of us will remember this afternoon when we took such a deep look into the heart of a Friend.

There were first of all the 12 men He had picked out of a crowd. They were chosen by himself. They didn't know it at the beginning, but they were meant to be His friends. One day He would say so clearly and unmistakably to them, "No longer do I call you servants . . . but I have called you friends" (John 15:15). As we turn the pages of the Gospels, we see Him deal with them. According to tradition, Thomas and Judas were a little more educated, but the others seem to have been fishermen except for one, who was a tax collector. And their friend was the Son of God! What a time He had opening their minds to His revolutionary ideas; stopping them from being materialistic, from grabbing immediate reward; getting them out of their smallish provincialism with its "What will people say?" into the worldwide outlook of "Go therefore and make disciples of *all* nations" (Matt. 28:19), and "And I tell you my, friends, do not fear those who kill the body, and after that have no more that they can do" (Luke 12:4).

Sometimes He gets really exasperated when they don't seem to get the point. "O faithless and perverse generation, how long am I to be with you?" (Matt. 17:17.) With their boats and nets they were certainly used to a hard life. They soon found out, however, that when they gave up everything they had been doing so far in order to follow Him, they were just going from one kind of hard work to another. Their Lord and Master, as they called Him at that time, was himself the most hard-working man they had ever met, day and night, seven days a week — whenever anybody needed Him. Isn't it somewhat significant that they said, "Lord, teach us to pray" (Luke 11:1), but never, "Lord, teach us to work." There were no days off, and unending hours of work. He never set up headquarters with an office and office hours in Jerusalem or Capernaum, where the people could have come to see Him. He was always on the go after the lost sheep. What vast distances He would cover, either in tropical heat or torrential rains! And what He did, He expected of His friends. Peter remembered it after 30 long years. Often they were so rushed they didn't even have time to eat!

At the same time, Jesus noticed what was going on,

and once we see Him taking a rest. They had just gotten the news that John the Baptist had been killed. Our Lord's heart was then so filled with sympathy towards His friends (some of whom had first been disciples of John), that He said: "Come away by yourselves . . . and rest a while" (Mark 6:31). How gratefully must they have crowded into Peter's boat and taken a picnic lunch along and begun to row over the lake expecting a quiet weekend. But the crowd had outwitted them. The people saw what was going on, ran along the shore, and arrived before the boat. Immediately our Lord forgot His own exhaustion and began to talk to the people, and of course, He expected the same of His friends. Finally He even told them to feed that big crowd (about five thousand). All we know from the Gospel is that the 12 had to minister to the people, and distribute bread and fish until everyone was satisfied. We don't hear a word about what happened to them. Maybe when all their guests were happily gone, they could eat from the leftovers in the 12 baskets.

One of the toughest lessons for them must have been to realize that the time when they were in a safe business where one could calculate how much one would make and how one could build up for the future, was gone. We can see how worried they were about this fact when Peter asked our Lord outright just how much they were going to make for themselves. The answer was not encouraging. He was promised an ample reward after death. But they would not give up. Time and again they would come up with such questions. Two of them would even get their mother to make a petition, but then as before, it doesn't seem to get them anywhere. "Even as the Son of man came not to be served but to serve" (Matt. 20:28). "A disciple is not above his teacher" (Matt. 10:24).

All right. They had swallowed to some little extent this bitter pill. But couldn't the ministering be restricted to nice people? Never mind the poor and the sick, but outcasts like tax collectors, bad women, and Samaritans! Was it really necessary for a respectable, honorable man to mix with them? Obviously it was. And it didn't stop with talking to them, either. They had to learn to eat with them and learn from their Master, uncomfortable though they must have felt about it, how one can even understand and finally like and defend them. It must have been one of the minor shocks when they heard Him say, "Truly, I say to you, the tax collectors and the harlots go into the kingdom of God before you" (Matt. 21:31). Sometimes there seemed to be nothing refined about His taste.

All this time, however, their love for Him grew. So when our Lord would say on that fatal morning when many of the "nice" people turned their backs on Him, "Do you also wish to go away?" Peter could answer in the name of all: "Lord, to whom shall we go? You have the words of eternal life" (John 6:67–68). The great love and patience He had lavished on them were bearing fruit.

They must have been courageous men if they had worked on the Sea of Galilee. This big lake is famous and feared for the sudden squalls which arise. The people say that Lake Champlain, which is not very far from us in Stowe, has an ugly temper. That's what people felt toward the Sea of Galilee. Now these men had to learn a new kind of courage. "Behold, we are going up to Jerusalem," He would say to them one day, "and everything that is written of the Son of man by the prophets will be accomplished" (Luke 18:31). And knowing all these dangers now, they still had to go. They were constantly mixed up with the priests and Pharisees, whom their Master almost seemed to provoke. One almost sees them wince when He had to cure somebody again on the Sabbath, knowing already the inevitable outcome.

With all His great love and endless patience, and in spite of their slow-growing understanding, once in a while

He had to scold them. For instance, when they one day didn't want mothers to bring their children to Him; or the crushing retort when Peter, meaning so well, advised Him to stay away from Jerusalem.

And all the while they didn't have a steady income. They lived on alms. They had no income. They were worse off than the fox who had his den and the birds who had their nests — they had no security. And still we never hear them really complain. Sometimes they quarrel among themselves, not infrequently they behave stupidly, but they always appreciate that what He is asking of them is not even a small particle of what He demands of himself.

Here I looked up and met Hester's eyes smiling at me.

"Where is it, Hester?" I asked.

"At home in the file 'Mother Private,' " she answered, "but I know it. Do you want to hear it?" And Hester, having recently typed up that little poem of which we spoke now because we thought it so nicely fitting, recited:

REPARTEE
by Alfred Barrett (1906–1985)

Because her bucking cart-mule
Showed scant respect for a saint,
There rose from a ditch near *Medina
Del Camp* this complaint.

"Why do you treat me thus, dear Lord?
I'd willingly shed my blood,
But I balk at the prospect of martyrdom
In this Castilian mud!"

Smiled Christ — "Thus do I treat My friends,
So, must I thus treat you. . . ."
"No wonder, Lord," sighed Teresa,
"No wonder You have so few."[1]

Everybody laughed except Peter. He didn't even listen, but stared, fascinated, into his New Testament. Peter had been a navy officer in the war, and he is our second oldest friend in America. The navy always finds the navy, and so he had become a special friend of my husband. We will never forget how we met him. It was on a day in September, a really unpleasant, wet, foggy, cold New England autumn day. It was our first summer in Stowe on the farm where the old house had fallen in and we camped in tents and barns doing as much work on the farm as we possibly could. On this day we had just finished digging the potatoes out and were now sorting them in a shed when a young navy officer climbed up our hill, clad in immaculate white, bringing greetings from Michael, a mutual friend. After the exchange of the first few polite phrases the incautious young man said, "Is there anything I could help do to help?" Off he went in overalls to the potatoes.

For years to come we would have to listen to his funny descriptions of his aching back. Having a wonderful sense of humor, he very soon became famous for his storytelling. When the war was over and Peter wanted to go back into his former business, he met our Lord, who said, "Come, follow Me." Unlike the rich young man, he sold everything he had and went and followed Him; and so the elegant young navy officer was now a seminarian. As he looked up from his book, there was a different expression on his face. His usually laughing eyes had a new and almost tender light.

"Please look up John," he said, "beginning with the 13th chapter. If we have found out so far what He did with His friends, here we seem to learn how He really felt about them."

We looked and — Peter was right. What a different language! One almost wonders whether this is the same person who had exclaimed a few pages before, "How long am I to be with you?" when He says now:

Little children, yet a little while I am with you (John 13:33).

Let not your hearts be troubled; believe in God, believe also in me (John 14:1).

If you ask anything in my name, I will do it. If you love me, you will keep my commandments (John 14:14–15).

I will not leave you desolate; I will come to you (John 14:18).

He who has my commandments and keeps them, he it is who loves me; and he who loves me will be loved by my Father, and I will love him and manifest myself to him (John 14:21).

If a man loves me, he will keep my word, and my Father will love him, and we will come to him and make our home with him (John 14:23).

These things I have spoken to you, while I am still with you. But the Counselor, the Holy Spirit, whom the Father will send in my name, he will teach you all things, and bring to your remembrance all that I have said to you. Peace I leave with you; my peace I give to you (John 14:25–27).

Let not your hearts be troubled, neither let them be afraid (John 14:27).

As the Father has loved me, so have I loved you; abide in my love. If you keep my commandments, you will abide in my love, just as I have kept my Father's commandments and abide in his love (John 15:9–10).

These things I have spoken to you, that my joy may be in you, and that your joy may be full. This is my commandment, that you love one another as I have loved you. Greater love has no man than this, that a man lay down his life for his friends. You are my friends if you do what I command you. No longer do I call you servants, for the servant does not know what his master is doing; but I have called you friends, for all that I have heard from my Father I have made known to you (John 15:11–15).

In the world you have tribulation; but be of good cheer, I have overcome the world (John 16:33).

We had long stopped looking at our books but were listening to Peter's ringing voice solemnly reading this story of the greatest friendship the world has ever seen. But the greatest was still to come when our Lord, after having opened His Heart to His friends, raising His eyes to heaven, said to His Father:

I have manifested thy name to the men whom thou gavest me out of the world; thine they were, and thou gavest them to me, and they have kept thy word. Now they know that everything that thou hast given me is from thee . . . and they have believed that thou didst send me. I am praying for them; I am not praying for the world but for those whom thou hast given me (John 17:6–9).

I do not pray for these only, but also for those who believe in me through their word, that they may all be one; even as thou, father, art in me, and I in thee (John 17:20–21).

Father, I desire that they also, whom thou hast given me, may be with me where I am (John 17:24).

A deep long silence followed. It was not uncomfortable; it was rather a happy and satisfied silence. As we looked down on the treetops at our feet far out into the valley over to Mount Mansfield or, lying on our backs, up into the deep blue sky, the word started working in our hearts: "I do not pray for these only, but also for those who believe in me through their word." And with deep gratitude in our hearts, we understood that this meant us.

An indescribable happiness wells up in the heart when one realizes that this is the way He talks about His friends to the Father, even if He foresees that soon they will be scattered in their houses and leave Him alone. Thus enveloped and protected, the feeling of greatest peace — modern man calls it security — settles in the soul. With great eagerness one wishes, however, to make absolutely sure that one belongs to this inner circle. That's why it is so good to know that He said, "You are my friends if you do what I command you." And a moment later, "This is my commandment, that you love one another."

CHAPTER
16

"HE ... HEALED THEM"

O nce again we were sitting in the bay window with another family, very close friends of ours, Paul and Mary and their three oldest children, and Father Wasner. Paul is a doctor, and the conversation turned towards miracles.

"Not so long ago," said Mary; "we had five doctors and their wives for dinner. On that evening we had a lively discussion of miracles. Paul and I have wanted ever since to look up all the miracles of our Lord, but we haven't gotten around to it. Would it perhaps be possible ... ?"

In a short time we were busy turning pages again, Mary listing the headlines:

> The wedding of Cana
> Cure of the official's son
> Exorcism of a demonic
> Peter's mother-in-law

The draught of fishes
Cure of a leper
Cure of a paralytic
Cure of a withered hand
"Lord, I am not worthy. . . ."
The widow of Nain
The storm on the lake
Geraza
The daughter of Jairus
The woman with the hemorrhage
Cure of two blind and one mute
The pool of Bethsaida
Feeding of five thousand
Feeding of four thousand
Walking on the water
The Syro-Phoenician woman
Cure of the deaf-mute
Cure of the blind
The Transfiguration
Cure of the lunatic boy
The money in the mouth of the fish
The man born blind
The paralytic in Capernaum
The stooped woman
The man with the dropsy
The ten lepers
Lazarus
His own Resurrection
Mass cures: "He . . . healed them."

Every one of those stories had been read aloud. Now we looked up at the list, and quite naturally, miracles seemed to group themselves. There were cures; there were exorcisms; there were miracles of nature, like the storm on the lake and His walking on the water; there were miracles of a completely supernatural character like the happenings of Jesus' baptism, the Transfiguration, and the Resurrection.

One of the youngsters suggested that we write the headlines of each one on a little card so that we could group them on the table. We did.

The large group of cures was subdivided very soon into cures which happened through touching and others which took place through a mere act of His will. We found that while "He laid his hands on every one of them and healed them" (Luke 4:40), sometimes He says to the suffering ones, "Go," and the miracle happens after their departure. Once He says to an official whose son was sick in another town, "Go; your son will live" (John 4:50). Another time He goes into quite a long ceremony with the deaf and dumb (Mark 7:32–35).

It was fascinating. Everybody plunged into the discussion. Everybody found a new angle. Quite naturally, everybody found questions to ask. "Why does He sometimes touch a person and sometimes not? Why does He go into ceremonies when He proved that He can change water into wine by merely willing it, without even saying so? And . . . and . . . and. . . ."

It was one of those days when the supper bell found us still sitting in the bay window. None of us had noticed the time flying, and questions were by no means all answered. Letters went back and forth whenever one of the two families found a new angle for an answer. The questions have still not all been solved. What a great consolation that Augustine says that what he does not know about the Gospels is so much more that what he does know!

Another time the topic was our Lord as a storyteller. We picked out all the parables one by one.

> The story of the prodigal son
> "A sower went out to sow"
> The laborers in the vincyard
> The ten virgins
> The story of the Good Samaritan
> The story of the rich man and Lazarus

And so on. In looking at them more closely, we could see great differences among them according to the audiences our Lord was addressing.

Then came the questions: "Why did He talk in parables at all? Why did He explain them at times, and at other times, not?" Quite naturally, we people of today, the age of the short story, will admire such immortal masterpieces of storytelling as the Prodigal Son or the Good Samaritan.

Automatically this discussion led to another one — our Lord as a teacher. There we see Him in the Sermon on the Mount instructing the multitudes, instructing communities, and every so often instructing His disciples. He always followed a completely new method, His very own, so that the people said in admiration, "No man ever spoke like this man!" (John 7:46). "For He taught them as one who had authority, and not as their scribes" (Matt. 7:29). It was not only the method which was so new, but most of all, it was *what* He was teaching.

For the first time people listened to the greatest news of all that there is a Father in heaven so closely concerned about every one of them that not even a hair can fall from their heads without His knowing it.

For the first time also people listened to another piece of news. That because they are all children of the same "Father who art in heaven" (Matt. 6:9) they must feel like sisters and brothers among each other: "Love your neighbor as yourself" (Matt. 19:19, 22:39, etc.).

For the first time they learned how they could themselves attain their Father's kingdom: "The kingdom of God is at hand; repent, and believe in the gospel" (Mark 1:15).

For the first time they learned about spiritual life and how to nourish it, and how to regain it after it has been lost.

For the first time they learned how to become happy — not by winning friends and influencing people, but by becoming poor in spirit and, pure in heart: "Blessed are . . ." (Matt. 5:3–11).

There is no end to the new facets one can find on the divine crystal, Jesus as a teacher.

But the same can be said about our Lord as a leader, especially to us, the children of our times with their self-appointed duces, fuehrers, and leaders.

"I couldn't imagine Christ or His mother ever having gone to a party," exclaimed a lady once. Well, if we can't imagine that, we had better look into the pages of the New Testament quickly. He went whenever He was invited, and that seems to have been quite frequently. Much too often for the taste of the Pharisees, who finally called Him disgustedly "a glutton and a drunkard" (Matt. 11:19). At the wedding of Cana we see Him and His mother attending one of those Oriental weddings which lasted at least a week, where there was entertainment for the guests in the form of dancing and music and speeches, much good food, and even more good wine. It is very profitable to do some research work on our Lord at parties. It makes Him so much more human.

Maria von Trapp

"O Woman, Great Is Your Faith"

S ome years ago I gave a lecture in a large city. During
the talk it happened several times that you could have
heard that famous pin drop. Afterwards there was a
little party, and there I was offered the chance of a lifetime.
A rich lady approached me and said, "If you talk like that,
then you can also found a church."

She pleaded with me to found a church solely for
women and be its first high priestess. Money would not matter. One million dollars would be available right away. I could
also design my own vestments.

This was like a bombshell. A lively discussion followed.
She complained bitterly that all the existing churches were
catering to men. "Just look at your own church," she
frowned. "The pope, bishops, priests — always men. Women
have nothing to say during the service. That goes back to
the time when Christ chose only men for His disciples. He
is to be blamed for it all. He brought women to submission

159

under men. He enslaved them as they had never been enslaved before in history. Just remember the beautiful temple services of pagan times," she exclaimed with enthusiasm, "where the high priestess conducted worship and music. We absolutely have to bring those times back!"

When I had made it unmistakably clear that she could not count on me, since I was already a member of what she had called my church and also because I didn't believe what she said myself, she was disappointed and angry. "How undignified for a woman to follow Christ!" were her last words.

When I met my family, they didn't want to believe me at first. It sounded so absurd. I had been taken completely by surprise, as much by the suggestion that I found a church as by the accusations against Christ and Christianity, and I couldn't even retaliate. I knew it was silly and wrong, but I had never done too much thinking on that point. Now we all agreed that there was a great need for some real research on Christ and women.

We had to begin by finding out about the "good old times" before Christ. Father Wasner got the respective historical books from the public library, and now we studied the position of women among the old Greeks, among the Romans, among the Egyptians, the Buddhists, and the Confucians. The more we read, the more we found that women were the property of men. Fathers or husbands could sell them or kill them. Men were "wisdom personified" whereas women were born stupid, a mere zero for mankind. Nowhere in all the pagan lands and religions was there any respect for women. Classical paganism had done away completely with dignity of womanhood.

It was somewhat different among the ancient Jews. Whereas the pagans of antiquity glorified promiscuity, the Jews of the Old Testament always called a sin a sin. Marriage and family were held in high esteem. But the women themselves had just as little to say as their sisters among the pagans. The father gave his daughters in marriage without asking them. Women were restricted to running the household and caring for the little children. They were not worthy of being educated or of partaking in any of the religious ceremonies. At the time of Christ their position had become much worse. Women at that time were rather things than persons. The rabbis couldn't insist enough on the superiority of the men. Women were inferior. They could not be legal witnesses. Women, slaves, and children were on the same level. To study the Torah — the law of the Old Testament — was the exclusive privilege of men. A famous rabbi coined this expression: "Rather should the Torah be burned than given in trust to a woman." The rabbis said that one hundred women were the equivalent of two men. (That was already a great improvement on the famous Euripides, who said that ten thousand women were worth less than one man.) At the time of Christ the people of Israel had lost the ways of old when they had venerated Deborah, Esther, Ruth, Rebekah, and Rachel. Just like her pagan sister, woman was sighing in her degradation for the coming Messiah in a twofold way — for all her people and for women especially.

This was the state of affairs when the time was fulfilled. This was now the time of "the woman." When everything had been spoiled for men in paradise, God himself had pronounced this prophecy addressed to the serpent: "I will put enmities between thee and the woman" (Gen. 3:15). The great rabbis, teachers, and scribes did not know that when a certain little child was born in Nazareth, He was conceived without sin and His mother would be addressed by the angel, "Hail, full of grace." Mary was "the woman" who would restore her sex to the dignity of the time before the Fall. Her Son would bring about this revolution which would reinstate women and place them at the side of men as it was in paradisiacal times when God said, "It is not good that man should be alone; I will make him a helper *comparable to him*" (Gen. 2:18;NKJV).

After He had grown up and had lived under the same roof for 30 long years with the holiest of women, He who was the Son of God, but also the Son of Man — her Son — had the greatest respect for her whole sex. And when the time had finally come for Him to talk about the things His Father had told Him, this was among these things: that before God the soul of a woman is worth exactly as much as the soul of a man. He would teach this truth not only in words, but also by His actions.

This is one of the most revolutionary deeds in the three long years of His public life — that He will address women just as much as men. The rabbis taught that a man was not even supposed to greet a woman, not even so much as look at her on the street. He had to avert his eyes. If he had bad luck and had, for instance, to ask directions from a woman, he had to do it with the fewest possible words, eyes lowered. Not only should a man not talk *with* a woman, but he should also not mention them at all in his speech. Now there comes our Lord. Every so often He chose His parables from the world of women as well as from the world of men.

For instance, after He had just likened the kingdom of Heaven to "a grain of mustard seed which a *man* took" He would liken it to "leaven which a *woman* took and hid in three measures of flour, till it was all leavened" (Matt. 13:31–33).

After He had painted the beautiful picture of the Good Shepherd who went tirelessly after the lost sheep, He immediately told about the woman having ten drachmas and losing one. Did she not "light a lamp and sweep the house and seek diligently until she finds it?" (Luke 15:8). Another time the kingdom of heaven will be like ten virgins (Matt.25:1–13).

When He wants to tell them a parable — that they must pray always and not lose heart (Luke 18:1) He tells them the story of the widow and the unjust judge.

"And he sat down opposite the treasury, and watched the multitude putting money into the treasury" (Mark 12:41). This is the second time that He places a widow as an example before His disciples. The first widow has surmounted all obstacles with her persistent heart (Luke 18:1–5). The second one will be praised for her final generosity. "She out of her poverty has put in everything she had, her whole living" (Mark 12:44).

On that same Tuesday when our Lord is teaching in the temple and has just told the beautiful story of the widow's mite, the Sadducees also come with a "widow story" — "the wife of the seven brothers" (Matt. 22:23–27). The answer they get they have most certainly not expected: that the woman as well as her seven husbands will be equal to the angels. This is so terrific that the Gospel says, "And no one was able to answer him a word, nor from that day did any one dare to ask him any more questions" (Matt. 22:46).

On that same day He tells them the story of the father with the two sons. The father said to the fist son, "Son, go and work in the vineyard today," but the boy said he didn't want to. Afterwards he was sorry and went. The father went and said the same thing to the second son, who answered, "I go, sir," but he did not go. Then He asks the question: "Which of the two did the father's will?" His unwilling audience has to say the first. And now He says the hard words: "Truly, I say to you, the tax collectors and the harlots go into the kingdom of God before you. For John came to you in the way of righteousness, and you did not believe him, but the tax collectors and the harlots believed him; and even when you saw it, you did not afterward repent and believe him" (Matt. 21:28-32).

Another time He threatens them that "The queen of the South will arise at the judgment with this generation and condemn it; for she came from the ends of the earth to hear the wisdom of Solomon, and behold, a greater than Solomon is here" (Matt. 12:42).

In His own hometown He also starts talking about a widow, the widow of Sarepta. We know that His people got so angry about it that they tried to kill Him (Luke 4:25–29).

When He warns His listeners to be watchful because "you know neither the day nor the hour" (Matt. 25:13), He warns the men, "Then two men will be in the field; one is taken and one is left." Then He warns the women, "Two women will be grinding at the mill; one is taken and one is left" (Matt 24:40–41).

On the last day He tries to explain to them because they don't understand, "When a woman is in travail she has sorrow, because her hour has come; but when she is delivered of the child, she no longer remembers the anguish, for joy that a child is born into the world" (John 16:21).

And then came the Sabbath on which something happened which led to a climax. Luke tells us the story.

> And there was a woman who had had a spirit of infirmity for eighteen years; she was bent over and could not fully straighten herself. And when Jesus saw her, he called her and said to her, "Woman, you are freed from your infirmity." And he laid his hands upon her, and immediately she was made straight, and she praised God. But the ruler of the synagogue, indignant because Jesus had healed on the sabbath, said to the people,

"There are six days on which work ought to be done; come on those days and be healed, and not on the sabbath day." Then the Lord answered him, "You hypocrites! Does not each of you on the sabbath untie his ox or his ass from the manger, and lead it away to water it? And ought not this woman, a daughter of Abraham whom Satan bound for eighteen years, be loosed from this bond on the sabbath day?" As he said this, all his adversaries were put to shame; and all the people rejoiced at all the glorious things that were done by him (Luke 13:11–17).

"DAUGHTER OF ABRAHAM!" To call Abraham one's father was the great pride of every Jew; but all over the Scriptures there is talk only of the sons of Abraham. It was our Lord's very own invention to use the words "a daughter of Abraham." What a deep impression it made on His listeners. The ones were put to shame while the others rejoiced.

If a man was supposed to not even talk with a woman, how much less was he supposed to touch one? But there we see Jesus taking Peter's mother-in-law by the hand and curing her from the fever, and also taking Jairus' daughter who had died and giving her back to her parents. He who could say to one leper, "I will, be clean" (Mark 1:41) and he was made clean — He did not have to touch the women. No, He wanted to.

And how He shows His emotions for women! Out of compassion for a mother who is a widow, He raises her only son from the dead. Out of compassion for two sisters who are among His best friends, He calls forth their brother, who was four days in the tomb.

One of the most revolutionary things He ever did

happened in Samaria when His disciples found Him talking to the woman at Jacob's Well. Not only was He talking
to a woman, but she was also a Samaritan. Not only was
He talking to her, but He had also accepted a drink of
water at her hand. And not only that, but He finally dis-
closed His identity to her. And the first one to whom He
himself said that He was the Messiah was this sinful
stranger (John 4:4–42).

The Apostles really thought they were doing the right
thing when they told the mothers harshly to go away with
their little ones. After all, weren't they women? Unmistakably, our Lord taught them that they were still thinking in
the ways of old, whereas He had already founded the New
Covenant (Mark 10:13–16).

No rabbi would have defiled himself in talking to a
woman taken in adultery (John 8:1–11). No rabbi would
have allowed a sinful woman to touch his feet, to anoint his
head (Luke 7:37–50). No rabbi would have allowed a girl to
sit in at his talks to the men, and of all things, to sit right at
his feet. He also would have never allowed her sister to break
in and interrupt him in the middle of his speech. Still, Mary
and Martha were His closest friends (Luke 10:40–42).

The poor, elderly lady who had spent all her fortune
on doctors but couldn't be helped, must have heard about
His great kindness to women, because she said to herself, *If
I only touch His garment, I shall be healed,* and she approached Him in the crowd and touched the hem of His
garment (Luke 8:43–48).

His unequalled reputation traveled even across the
border to the country of the Syro-Phoenicians. A mother
from that country dared to approach Him, although she
knew what the Jews in general thought about Gentiles. Then
we see our Lord putting her off as He had once done, it
seems, to His mother. This woman, also could not be

cheated, and the final outcome was that Jesus not only did what she asked of Him, but also praised her: "O woman, great is your faith" (Matt. 15:21–28).

Therefore, we cannot be the least bit astonished when we see how women all over the country responded to the Master. A number of them even got together and, in a little club, followed Him around wherever He went. Not only that, but they took care of His and the disciples' needs. "And the twelve were with him, and also some women who had been healed of evil spirits and infirmities: Mary, called Magdalene, from whom seven demons had gone out, and Joanna the wife of Chuza, Herod's steward, and Susanna, and many others, who provided for them out of their means" (Luke 8:1–3).

The sober, critical men needed a direct invitation: "Come, follow me," and after they had done so, they would still quarrel among themselves as to which one would be the greater and wonder a good deal about their reward. As Peter worded it, "Lo, we have left everything and followed you. What then shall we have?" (Matt. 19:27) Women are different, although they also must have received a special vocation, because our Lord said once, "No man can come to me unless the Father who sent me draws him" (John 6:44), and another time, "You did not choose me, but I chose you" (John 15:16).

That was true of the women as well as of the men in the company. All they needed, however, was the permission to stay with Him. He didn't have to give them special rewards. He knew all they wanted was to be allowed to love Him and to show their love by providing for Him. What they did was quite unusual. Their contemporaries surely couldn't have understood it. They were obviously from different walks of life. Some were noble ladies who would have left everything behind and would follow in

His footsteps. This is the first real feminine movement.

Up and down throughout Galilee they followed Him and at the end they would be under the cross. They would help to bury Him, and they would want to mourn at His grave. Little wonder it is, therefore, that after the Resurrection, our Lord appears to the women. First, tradition tells us, to His mother, and then to Mary Magdalene (Mark 16:9).

This is a true story as it is written down in the pages of history. Against the dark background of the position of women in ancient and modern paganism, Christ stands out as a figure of light. Mathilda Ludendorff, one of the leading names among the Nazis, wrote a book in which she tried to prove that Christ is only a myth, and His teachings only ancient wisdom from India plagiarized by the Gospels. Her husband, a famous name of his time, introduced this book with the following recommendation: "On the widespread reading of this book depends the liberation of the individual, of the German people, and of all peoples." The title of the book was *Redemption from Jesus Christ*. And her sister in America has said it was undignified for women to follow Christ. Mary Magdalene, however, says in the name of all her sisters throughout the centuries, " 'I have seen the Lord'; and she told them that he had said these things to her" (John 20:18).

CHAPTER
18

"THE WOMAN"

It was at the end of the summer, and our music camp was just over. A few of our best friends had stayed behind to help us close up. The evenings we usually spent in my little house on the campus sitting around in a circle, bay window-fashion, talking about "it." "It" is spiritual life, which has many more aspects than there are evenings to talk them over.

Stanislaus, one of our seminarian friends, leaned back in his chair and said rather helplessly, "I don't know what I can do. I have absolutely no feeling for Mary. Try as I may — I have read many books about her — she seems to me a perfect stranger. She is so completely unreal. That makes me so sad, but what can one do?"

We had spent so much time with the Holy Family in Nazareth, seeing the mother of the house as a real house-wife, cooking, washing, baking bread, cleaning house, preparing and mending garments, and all the while mothering a little boy. Now we told Stanislaus all about it. How very, very real she was!

Then we came to talk about one of the most beautiful stories in all the Gospels, the one of the marriage feast in Cana in Galilee, when Mary, the mother of Jesus, was there. The gospel continues, "Jesus also was invited" (John 2:2). At that time He had not made a name for himself yet. He and His disciples were obviously invited on account of His mother, to whose family the newlyweds must have belonged. Mary is usually described in word and picture as a rather shy, retiring person, clad in complete silence. The faraway look in her eyes indicates that she was pondering in her heart, which seems to make her oblivious to what is going on around her. All these artists of pen and brush seem to feel it a sacrilege to let her stoop down so low as the little trifles of everyday life. As the words of Holy Scriptures are inspired by the Holy Ghost, we can confidently take the story of the wedding of Cana as a most valuable aid to a true biography of Mary.

"When the wine failed, the mother of Jesus said to him . . ."(John 2:3). To appreciate what that means we have to understand all the customs of such a marriage feast of her time, how the friend of the bridegroom was the steward who was also in charge of the wine, and who was most solicitous that everything should go as well as possible. It had escaped his attention, but it had not escaped her motherly vigilance. What really happened is this. Through the thoughtlessness of somebody, the wine was alarmingly short, which would amount to a great embarrassment for the hosts. Mary does not think this is a trifle too little to bother her Son with. As a real housewife, as a real mother, she foresees this painful situation.

She must have been up and around, coming and going, watching and seeing everything, and before anybody else, she anticipated the need and "did something about it." How heart-warming! And again, how real and how close she becomes. When her Son in His answer, which does not sound encouraging to us, but didn't disturb her a bit, calls her "Woman," many people like Stanislaus wonder and don't understand. So we mentioned that last day in Eden to Stanislaus, when God Almighty himself gives her this greatest of all titles in His prophecy about "the woman" (Gen. 3:15).

And what authority she had! As was usually the case, the women belonging to the wedding party assembled at the house days ahead of time baking and preparing. Maybe Mary had taken over the leadership among them. With what natural poise she now steps over to the servants and commands, "Do whatever he tells you" (John 2:5). Perhaps the servants may have laughed outright at the funny idea of filling those huge stone jars with water at the end of a feast when there would be no more ablutions; but because of her words, they went back and forth many times with their pitchers, filling the jars. Doesn't she still do the same thing today? Looking imploringly at us, she says, "Do whatever He tells you." How can we refuse her pleading and not listen to Him when He says, "Love one another as I have loved you" (John 15:12).

Stanislaus had already said repeatedly that this was all new to him, and it had never occurred to him in just that way. He seemed to grow happier and the tense, anxious expression on his face vanished visibly.

While we were telling and explaining, I got one of those fits against this degenerate sacred art of Barclay Street. How could a young man of our days get any access to a person represented in these doll-like faces, clad in pastel colors, whose lily-white hands seem only meant to be folded but couldn't be imagined as kindling a fire or washing a little boy's clothes or taking care of a carpenter's household. It seems to me that heresies don't absolutely have to be preached or printed; they can also be painted or carved in stone. These cute and sweet representations of Mary are a heresy widely spread.

And then we came to the end of the Gospels. We see Mary as a warm-blooded woman, mothering not only her own child but anyone who was in need. When it comes to the passion of our Lord, the Holy Ghost lets us have a look into the depths of her heart. "Did you not know?" her Son had said to her once when she hadn't quite understood Him. That had been 21 years ago. In those years she had been pondering in her heart on everything He had said and done.

We see her now in the most cruel suffering a mother can endure: her Son caught like a criminal, betrayed by one of His own, denied by one of His best friends, mocked, ridiculed, and treated with the utmost scorn, scourged, tortured, disfigured, and finally condemned to death. Mary knew what power as a mother she might have over human hearts, how irresistible she would be if she were to step up to Pilate who was wavering anyhow, how she could perhaps turn the fury of the multitudes into pity.

She understood. And while her heart was pierced by the sword, she kept silently in the background. Simon was allowed to help carry the cross; the women could show their grief so that He even stopped and addressed them — the mother could only exchange a silent look. Then when the Gospel says, "Now there stood by the cross of Jesus his mother. . . . he saith unto his mother, Woman, behold thy son!" (John 19:25–26), it was the final approval of Jesus towards His mother. The prophecy was fulfilled. Here she stands: the woman.

CHAPTER
19

"CHRIST . . . LIVES IN ME"

In the beginning of the book I told you how it happened that we became interested in the life of Christ, in reconstructing it for ourselves as closely as possible, day by day, as it may have happened 1,900 years ago. Then in the next chapters I tried to tell how we did what we did by showing you some of our versions of the childhood story and the hidden life. Then I picked at random some of the countless aspects of our Lord's personality through which He was observed when we read the Gospels together throughout the years, alone and with our friends.

Now I want to tell you about still another discovery which we made when we had already become quite familiar with our Lord. This happened when one blessed day we seemed to understand what Paul meant when he exclaimed, "Jesus Christ is the same yesterday and today and for ever" (Heb 13:8;KJV); and in another place: "It is no longer I who live, but Christ who lives in me" (Gal. 2:20). These two statements were linked with the tremendous statement the mysterious voice had made to Paul when he was still Saul, "I am Jesus, whom you are persecuting" (Acts 9:5). From that day on these words became the whole pattern for our life.

If He can be identified with each one of us and *if* He is the same yesterday as today — then He just continues His very life in every one of us until the end of time.

It is a big moment when one realizes that. One feels like saying, "All right, dear Lord, here are my hands and feet, eyes and ears, my lips and my heart — they are Yours." I suppose this is the first step towards the final goal: "It is no longer I who live, but Christ who lives in me."

As soon as one becomes familiar with the fact that He is the same today as yesterday, one will meet Him constantly with His friends and stories. He really is the same. Nothing has changed. The Good Shepherd is still going after the lost sheep; the Father is still waiting for the Prodigal Son; Mary Magdalene is still sitting at His feet after He has freed her from seven devils.

It may be that not everybody will come across Mary Magdalene or the Good Shepherd in a drastic way. But as soon as we have awakened to what the words mean: "Jesus Christ . . . yesterday and today"; and as soon as we want to meet Him *today*, we can always find Him unerringly as Jesus, "a man of sorrows, and acquainted with grief" (Isa. 53:3). Once He would talk about the persecuted Christians of the first decade: "I am Jesus, whom you are persecuting" (Acts 9:5). This is true throughout the centuries. All we have to do is to learn to think about our fellow men in that term: "I am Jesus."

There are those incredible stories which seep through the Iron Curtain, which tell us how He re-lives His whole passion, how He is again scourged and crowned with thorns, "Despised and rejected by men" (Isa. 53:3), crucified and pierced by the lance. And this is not just one story, there must be thousands like it now.

If they seem a little remote to us, let us look around and we might find Him in the same persecutions He had to endure by the Pharisees: in our high schools and colleges, in offices, in newspapers and magazines. If we just learn to look, we shall find Him, and again He says, "I am Jesus, whom you are persecuting." As we look into the lives of our friends and neighbors, how much suffering do we find! And the great day will come when we discover the cross in our own life. Up to then we may have hated it, but on that glorious day we shall understand His words: "If any man would come after me, let him deny himself and take up his cross daily and follow me" (Luke 9:23). On that blessed day we shall suddenly know that it is He himself who wants to suffer in us, who wants to give us that greatest of all privileges: to help to "complete what is lacking in Christ's afflictions for the sake of his body, that is, the church" (Col. 1:24). This is a mystery as great as the Incarnation or the blessed Trinity. We shall never quite understand how it can be that we are called upon to co-operate in the work of the redemption, but so it is. We can only faintly understand it when we think of the body of Christ, of which He is the head and we are the members. And this whole body is suffering throughout the ages until the measure of suffering is fulfilled.

What we once said of Mary and Joseph, how they are still going from house to house seeking shelter, we can now say of the Son of Man. He is still carrying His cross, and we meet Him every day. Do we want to hold it with the scribes and elders, saying, "He is the King of Israel; let him come down now from the cross, and we will believe in him" (Matt. 27:42), or translated into our language, "If there were a God, there couldn't be this awful war. How can God allow so much unhappiness?"

Encountering Him TODAY we may come across fantastic situations but, after all, hasn't His whole life been full of such fantastic events, and haven't we discovered that His life is going on in our very days? So don't be astonished when, after you have studied the life of Christ in the land of Israel, you discover it again in Vermont, Chicago, New York, and other places.

Georg and Maria at home in Stowe.

CHAPTER
20

A LETTER

Stowe, Vermont
April 1951

Dear friends:

It was the end of January 1951. Our Christmas vacation was over, and the great blue bus came from New York to get us for our concert tour to the West Coast. There was the usual hustle and bustle of stowing all the many things into the bus, this time even a baby crib for Werner's little Barbara. There was the running back and forth with the last-minute errands. There was Dave blowing the horn and shouting "All aboard!" and when the bus finally rolled out of the courtyard, there was Martina standing on the porch next to her husband Jean, waving, half-happy, half-sad. This was the first time she would not be with us in all those many years of singing. That was sad. But when we came back from the West Coast at the end of April, there would be a little baby lying in the cradle upstairs. Martina had brought this old, wood-carved cradle along from Salzburg this past summer, and now she was fixing it for her first child. So this was a farewell with a tear and a smile.

Four weeks later we drove into one of those large, modern motor courts in Wasco, California. It was a Sunday night, the end of February. We had had an afternoon concert, after which we had driven on to the next concert town, and now we would have a quiet Sunday evening together. This and the fact that we all prefer these beautiful motor courts to any hotel put us in the best of spirits. The man at the desk in the office said that a long-distance call was waiting for us. When he said, "You should call Operator 14 in Morrisville, Vermont," we knew the call came from home. It must be something very urgent.

We placed a call, and very shortly afterward, the operator said: "Here is your party; go ahead."

And a voice at the other end sobbed into the telephone, "Mother — Martina is dead."

This is one of those moments where the heart actually seems to stop, and everything around one disappears in darkness.

The connection was not good, and all we could understand was that the baby had started to come four weeks too early, but the doctor was glad, because it was large. Martina was in the hospital. Everything went fine at the beginning until complications arose which made it necessary for the doctor to suggest an operation. The baby died right after it was baptized. Martina seemed all right. The operation was over, the doctors were gone. Martina was just beginning to wake up from the anaesthetic, when all of a sudden, her heart stopped. And could we come home now, please?

Meanwhile, the family had gotten settled in their different cottages, getting ready for a quiet Sunday evening.

Now I had to tell them. I sent little Johannes around with the message that everybody should come immediately to cabin #6.

We knelt down and prayed, all of us numb and still without understanding what that meant: Martina is dead.

Now we had to attend to practical matters: airplane tickets to Burlington. Dave, who was deeply shocked, went to the telephone and returned soon with the unexpected news: "Every space is taken. They can put you on the waiting list. The earliest chance will be in three days." That meant we had to give up the idea of all of us going home.

But I implored Dave, "Please try to get at least one seat for me." After hours of anxious waiting, one seat was secured, leaving Los Angeles at eight o'clock the next morning. But we were far from Los Angeles. I had to drive 50 miles to the next airport, from where a plane would take me at two o'clock in the morning down south. When I was getting ready to leave, the family gathered around me handing me letters "for Martina," as tears streamed down their faces. Father Wasner and Dave went along to the airport. Then — a last goodbye, a last blessing, and I was alone. There was a long night and a long day until the plane got into LaGuardia Field. One of our close priest friends was waiting for me.

"The connecting plane to Burlington has left already, and you have to stay overnight in New York. But tomorrow we shall come with you." I was deeply touched and very grateful in Martina's name when I learned that six priests would attend her funeral.

The closer the moment came when I should meet Jean and Pierre and Therese (Jean's brother and his wife) and Martina, the more I dreaded it. But when I finally stood at her side, looking down on her beautiful face, I felt a strange peace coming over me, which seemed to emanate from Martina. There she was lying where her father had lain before in our big living room in her wedding dress with an imperceptible, tiny smile around her lips. At her feet in a small white coffin slept little Notburga, her child.

And then we sat together, Jean and I, holding each other's hands. There was not very much to tell. The doctors didn't know themselves. Martina, who had never been sick in all her life, had been well to the very last moment. The doctors didn't even think that it was an embolism. They just frankly didn't know. A caesarian operation is usually nothing to worry about nowadays. It is being done successfully all the time.

"God wanted her," Jean said quietly. After a long silence he added, "She was too good to live very much longer. I had had that feeling often lately. She is in heaven." Poor Jean. He had been so happy, and now, in an instant, he had lost wife and child.

Then we had to attend to practical matters. Jean said, "Mother, let's do everything ourselves. I know Martina would want it that way." His two brothers, Pierre and Jacques, went out to the graveyard to dig the grave. First they had to clear away six feet of snow, which was lucky in a way, because the soil under so much snow was not frozen very deep. The end of February is still deepest winter and very cold in Vermont.

Jean and Martina had been helping Wayne, the carpenter, during the last weeks, finishing the new wing, and Wayne, like everybody else, had grown very fond of Martina and was, like everybody else, also deeply shocked. Jean asked Wayne now to make a coffin for Martina in old-world style out of white pine boards with a big cross on the lid, the cross stained dark. The funeral was set for Thursday at ten o'clock. I sent a telegram to the West Coast, where I knew that ten anxious hearts were waiting for news: "OUR DEAR MARTINA AND HER LITTLE NOTBURGA WILL BE

BURIED THURSDAY TEN O'CLOCK." I knew they would sing a requiem at the same time in California as we would in Stowe.

Telegrams and letters came, and flowers started pouring in, and friends arrived. There was always someone with Martina. Prayers were said in French, in German, in English. In spite of the bad road on our hill and of the bitter cold, people came from all around. The telephone rang constantly with people from the village offering their cars, their help. It was a great comfort in such bottomlessly sad hours to feel such compassion. In the evenings the living room was filled. During the day we gathered a couple of times in the bay window, looking over at Martina, rehearsing the Requiem High Mass. From a nearby college the choir had offered to sing it but — "Let's do everything ourselves," we had said. "Martina would like it better that way." With the singing family way out in California, I was a little bit worried as to how it would go, but when Father McDonnell arrived, who is choir director in his seminary, all was well, and I was sure Martina would like it.

On Wednesday Rupert came with Rosmarie, who had stayed with him, helping him around the house and with the children. Now there was at least one brother and one sister with Martina. With Rupert also came Anne Marie, one of his sisters-in-law.

In the evenings Father McDonough, our pastor, came over and gave a little talk on the liturgy of a Christian burial, which is so very consoling, and how the first Christians had looked at death. Instead of mourning, they celebrated a feast, the birthday of their beloved one in heaven. Instead of expressing their sympathy, they congratulated the bereaved. Some of this spirit we could feel descending upon us more and more.

On Wednesday the coffin arrived. We put it on the table

in the music room and lined it with fresh balsam twigs and flowers. In the evening after the last prayer was said, we all went in and, standing around the coffin, we said the Lord's Prayer for the next one in our midst to die. This is an old Tyrolean custom, and it is a real *momento mori*. It makes one realize in a very straight-to-the-point way that one day it will be for us.

Friends kept coming until past midnight. This is the mercy of these days. There are so many arrangements to be made, so many things to be thought about, and that, too, is a great help. Pierre and Therese, who had been married with Martina and Jean on the same day, really outdid themselves in arranging everything "as Martina would like it."

Jean dreaded the black hearse and was sure Martina would not like to be put in there, so Rupert and the others decorated our Jeep truck with carpets and evergreens. After a last prayer at Martina's side, all the friends went to get their coats, while we placed Martina on her last bed of flowers and fragrant balsam, placing little Notburga in the arm of her mother, covering them both with the rich folds of her bridal veil. Then we went down the hill to the little wooden church, at the threshold of which Father McDonough awaited Martina. As we entered the church, we sang: "*Subvenite sancti Dei, occurrite angeli Domini. . . .*" (Come, ye saints of God, meet us, oh angels of the Lord, take her soul and offer her to the presence of the Highest.) And now with the words and music of the Requiem we understood again what is meant by the words "Holy Mother Church." No one can console like a mother, and no one can console and help better than this great mother of us all, the church. "Eternal rest grant to her, Oh Lord," she says, "and may perpetual light shine upon her."

When we left the church, it was snowing in big white flakes, and when we came to the cemetery, the little mound of fresh dirt next to the grave was covered with a white blanket.

At the same time, the rest of the family went into the Catholic church in Coalinga, California, thinking they would quietly, all by themselves, sing a requiem; but when they arrived, the church was filled. Word had gotten around. All the school children had come, and many other people. And so it turned out to be a manifold "*Requiem eternam dona eis Domine*" which went up to the throne of God. At such moments one feels suddenly that this is what we meant when we say in the creed, we believe in the communion of saints; when all these perfect strangers turn into sisters and brothers, co-members of the church militant, uniting in prayer.

After we had all filed past the open grave, we went back to the house. Everybody was half-frozen. A roaring fire was kindled in the fireplace, and hot lunch was served.

In the morning mail was a letter from a very dear friend, Reverend Father Abbot of the Trappists. It said, "We envy you your sorrow and Martina her heaven."

As the snowstorm increased, many of the guests wanted to leave before it should be too difficult to get down the hill. I had to fly back the same night to San Francisco. Before leaving for the airport, I wanted to sit once more with Jean. He had been really wonderful all these days, so truly resigned to the will of God. Now he told me how Martina had used all the money I had sent her for her birthday two weeks before for Austrian relief packages. Jean said he would send all the baby things Martina had so lovingly prepared for little Notburga to Austria to be given to a very poor mother with the request to call the child Martin or Martina. That had been very hard to see — the nursery all prepared, the room next to their bedroom, with all those sweet little things lying around, waiting. I had been worried whether it wouldn't be too much for Jean to look at it from now on, so I asked him with a heavy heart what he planned to do next. He said he would go home to Montreal with his mother for a few days, and then he wanted to work hard and long hours, and so he intended to help that famous garden architect who had made that beautiful rock garden in front of our house. Working with rocks for the whole day, he thought he might be able to sleep. I felt greatly relieved. I knew how terribly quiet our big house could be when everybody is gone. That matters very little as long as there are two of you, but when the beloved is gone, never to return, then one discovers what "alone" means. For this there is no real remedy, but prayer and work help us to carry this cross.

And then I was on my way back to California in the airplane, alone with my thoughts. When Martina had been a little girl, she had said time and again, "I don't want to be grown-up ever. I always want to be little." God had really granted her that wish — outwardly and inwardly. That showed most in her uncomplicated, childlike piety. "We should be so continuously grateful for what God has done for us that the least we can give Him in return is all," she wrote once to Jean.

During the last years when I was quite sick, she had always taken care of me, spent weeks with me in the hospital and nursed me back to health, always patient, always cheerful, full of little surprises. A little bouquet of wild flowers, still wet with dew, picked at sunrise, or a handpainted little card, in which art she was a master. Once in those days she had confided to me that she was afraid to die. Now I had to think that God in His love and mercy had spared His child this last fright. He called her at the moment of her greatest happiness, when she expected to wake up and find her child in her arms. Now I tried to picture Martina's

real awakening, being greeted by her child, her mother and
father and little sisters and brothers. In my prayer book is a
card with the words of St. Jerome from a letter of consolation addressed to his friend, St. Paula, representing her dead
daughter Blesilla as saying, "Dear Mother, if you desire my
welfare, trouble not my peace and joy by your tears. You
fancy perhaps that I am lonely, but I live in such good company. I am with Mary the mother of our Lord and the holy
women mentioned in the Gospel. You pity me for leaving
the world, but now it is I rather who feel sorry for you and
all your family because you still linger in the prison of the
flesh and daily have to contend with the host of enemies
who are seeking to destroy you."

And on another one are the words of St. John
Chrysostom: "You complain that you suffer, having lost her
who was the joy of your life. Listen, my good friend. Suppose you had given your daughter in marriage to some good
and honorable man who went with her to a distant country
and made her rich and happy. Would not her happiness
soothe the grief you feel at the separation? How can you
dare to weep and refuse to be comforted, since your child
has been taken to himself by God our Lord and King, and
not by any earthly friend or relative?"

It was Friday late in the afternoon when I arrived in
San Francisco. When we approached the airport and I could
discover the people waiting for the airplane down there, I
looked for red stockings in the crowd, but there were none.
Then I looked for a Roman collar or a driver's cap, thinking that Father Wasner or Dave might have come, but there
was no collar and no cap to be seen. How would I get the 50
miles to Los Gatos, where we had the concert that night?
What a happy surprise it was then when an officer approached me with outstretched arms and a warm smile, and
I recognized Father Saunders, the army chaplain who had

for years helped us most generously in our Austrian relief work when he was stationed in Salzburg. While he was driving me to Los Gatos, I told him all about Martina, and then we talked about heaven.

I had just an hour to tell the family all about the last days, and then it was time for the concert. Afterwards Father Saunders joined us, and then at midnight, with the beginning of Saturday, we sang "Holy God, We Praise Thy Name," congratulating Martina on her true birthday.

The weeks passed, and when the concert tour was over, we returned home. There is an empty place at the family table now, and an empty room, and there is a fresh grave in the cemetery, which we visit every day. The wound is wide open again.

When the cross gets very heavy, it is good to remember what St. Aloysius Gonzaga wrote to his mother 11 days before his death: "I beg you, my honored Mother, be careful and don't withstand God's infinite goodness by bewailing as dead one who will live in God's presence. . . . Our separation will not last long. We shall see one another again in heaven and rejoice incessantly, being united with our Redeemer."

And now, my dear friends, we want to thank you also in Martina's name for all your prayers and words of comfort. Let us continue to pray for one another, especially for the one who will be next in our midst.

Yours gratefully,
The Trapp Family

It was about six weeks after Martina's death. We were at home by ourselves. It was in the evening at what we call our "social hour." We made up our family mind to spend the time between supper and evening prayer every night together around the fireplace, instead of vanishing into our different private quarters. We should really not have been in Stowe, but on the ship on the way to Australia. But the only one leaving from Vancouver was canceled, and for the second time, our tour to Australia and New Zealand was postponed. This unforeseen vacation we enjoy wholeheartedly. During the day we help finish the new wing, carpeting and painting, and in the evenings we spend a most comfortable hour together. Some are knitting or mending stockings, Verner is weaving belts on an ingenious handmade loom, which got him the nickname "Navajo Chief." Johannes is either whittling or playing with Flockie, his Airedale terrier. Father Wasner is copying music, which doesn't hinder him from listening to what is being talked about or read aloud, because he can do more than one thing at a time. I am either reading aloud from the day's mail, or knitting on Maria's sweater, a rather belated Christmas present.

On one of those evenings it was that Johannes suddenly asked, "Can Martina see us now?"

That started it.

"Yes," I said, "I'm sure she can. Aren't you?" And I looked questioningly from one to the other.

"Sure I am," said Lorli. "But what I want to know is how that works. If the body is buried, how can the soul see and hear?"

"Does Martina remember everything from her life here on earth, or — does she care to remember now?" asked Hedwig.

"And if she is in heaven now, exactly what might she be doing all the time?" inquired Johannes. "Can she play with her little baby, or does she have to stand before the throne of God all the time?"

"What do children do in heaven, the same as the grownups?"

"How would she recognize Father in heaven without a body?"

All of a sudden each single one of us discovered a great many burning questions inside, but just at this moment the bell rang for evening prayer in our chapel. Someone suggested looking into Holy Scriptures for whatever answers we could find. So we divided the different books of the New Testament among us, leaving the whole Old Testament to Father Wasner. Each one was to search his portion for whatever references he could find to life after death.

All of us say most earnestly every day when we recite the Apostle's Creed that "we believe in the resurrection of the body and life everlasting, amen." But now we had seen how many "what," "where," "when," and "how's" there are still left to ask. Together we now looked for the answers.

PART THREE

FOREVER

CHAPTER
21

BLESSED ARE THE DEAD

When we met again and each brought what he had found on "life everlasting" in the pages of Holy Scriptures, we were perfectly amazed at the amount to be found. If we only listed quotations, it would make many, many typewritten pages. Once the interest is aroused in "the last things" — death, judgement, heaven, and hell — one cannot stop pondering about it. We looked through our library. We found some highly interesting books: *In Heaven We Know Our Own,* by Blot; *What Becomes of the Dead* by Arendzen; and a little old-fashioned-looking book in German by Dr. Robert Klimsch: *Leben die Toten* ("Do the Dead Live" — a collection of sworn testimonies in beatification processes).[1]

When we talked these things over — not only in one evening but during weeks and months and ever since then, now and again — there were always two effects noticeable in the soul: first, a great consolation; and second, a greater

191

awareness of the fact that what we are pondering about now, we are going to meet one day. There is nothing really certain in our life — except death. This is the only thing I can really be sure of. I will die some day. And how will that be?

I am most grateful now for a personal experience of my own of some years ago: I *almost* died. I had been very sick, and now the end — as the doctor thought — had come. One understands that time is running short, and only in time can we do anything for Him, so every moment is precious to express one's love and one's complete resignation to the will of the Father.

People don't realize how cruel they are in their wrongly understood "consideration" when they keep the priest away as long as possible from their beloved sick in order "not to excite them." They don't know that they deprive their beloved ones of the greatest consolation. "Is any man sick among you?" writes James the Apostle. "Let him call for the elders of the church, and let them pray over him, anointing him with oil in the name of the Lord. And the prayer of faith will save the sick man, and the Lord will raise him up; and if he has committed sins, he will be forgiven" (James 5:14–15).

I was alone in the hospital in Vienna, my family hundreds of miles away sailing in the Adria. As I lay there with eyes closed, waiting for death, I heard the doctor say to the nurse that it wouldn't make any sense to try to contact the family. It was definitely too late for them to reach me. Although the doctor talked in a whisper, I could hear him very clearly. All my senses seemed to merge and concentrate into the one sense of hearing. I noticed that while I was opening my eyes wide, I could see nothing, although it was ten o'clock in the morning. Sight was gone. I heard the rustle of the sheets as the nurse removed them from the foot of my bed, and I heard her hand gliding over my feet and her voice when she said, "Her feet are already cold," but I couldn't feel it. Touch was gone.

I heard the doctor say he would give a camphor injection, and I heard the click of the needle; and although camphor has such a strong odor, I didn't smell it. That was gone.

"Am I dying?" I wanted to ask, but I couldn't move, couldn't speak. And then hearing also stopped, and there was a silence more intense than any silence I can remember. The body might have been helpless, but the soul was wide awake and in full possession of its faculties. Undisturbed by the outside, memory was keener than ever before. And in this anguish of a last agony the soul passed once more through it past life, seeing everything so much more clearly. Although nothing is to be seen, the soul senses very sharply the presence of an evil power which wants to influence it to give up: the sins are too many and too horrible to allow any hope. But it also senses another spiritual power present. It may be the guardian angel, soothing the soul, reminding it, "Though your sins are like scarlet, they shall be as white as snow" (Isa. 1:18): reminding the soul of the bottomless mercy and love of the Heavenly Father whom it is to meet very soon now.

And then? Well, I did not die. But for the rest of my life I shall be grateful for those most precious moments. The nurse told me afterwards that for a little while they thought I was already dead.

Afterwards I found out that this seems to be a general occurrence and not just my private experience. They say the senses die slowly, one by one. Therefore, we should take great care what is said and done in the presence of the dying. While they are fighting their last decisive battle, it would mean such a help if they could hear us talk to them about the mercy of God, about having trust and confidence. One day we shall have to take that same step, too. This might be the best preparation. And when everything is over and one of our beloved has died, we should remember the words of the Revelation of John: "I heard a voice from heaven saying, 'Write this: Blessed are the dead, who die in the Lord henceforth.' 'Blessed indeed,' says the Spirit, 'that they may rest from their labors, for their deeds follow them!' "(Rev. 14:13).

Maria with Johannes at the new lodge. (Photo: Yankee Images)

CHAPTER
22

THE JUDGMENT

A nd just as it is appointed for men to die once, and after that comes judgment" (Heb. 9:27), writes Paul to the Hebrews.

The Judgment! What do we know about it? We know that we shall face two different judgments, one immediately after death, the particular judgment, and one at the end of time, together with all mankind, the general judgment.

"Blessed are the pure in heart, for they shall see God" (Matt. 5:8). At the very moment after our death we see ourselves *exactly* as we are. If during the last moments while we were still breathing, our life has passed by in review, then after death our whole life is seen at once as in a flash, and it is seen *sub specie aeternitatis* — "as it will be seen for all eternity." Happenings and things which may have been of great value to us while we were alive may dwindle into nothingness, and what we had thought of as little trifles may take on giant significance. At this very moment we shall

perceive the justice of our future. The damned will be completely convinced that hell is the only place for them, and
saints will want to fly to God like a particle of iron to a
strong magnet.

At this decisive moment we shall not only be judged,
we shall also meet our judge. The righteous ones will meet
Him right away face to face. The damned will also recognize Him, and at the same instant they will want to flee
from Him in terror. Who will "the One" be: the Triune God,
or Christ?

Let us look at what Paul has to say:

> We would not have you ignorant, brethren,
> concerning those who are asleep, that you may
> not grieve as others do who have no hope. For
> since we believe that Jesus died and rose again,
> even so, through Jesus, God will bring with him
> those who have fallen asleep. For this we declare
> to you by the word of the Lord, that we who are
> alive, who are left until the coming of the Lord,
> shall not precede those who have fallen asleep.
> For the Lord himself will descend from heaven
> with a cry of command, with the archangel's call,
> and with the sound of the trumpet of God. And
> the dead in Christ will rise first; then we who are
> alive, who are left, shall be caught up together
> with them in the clouds to meet the Lord in the
> air; and so we shall always be with the Lord.
> Therefore comfort one another with these words
> (1 Thess. 4:13–17).

About the Last Judgment we are quite informed by
our Lord Jesus Christ himself.

When the Son of man comes in his glory, and all the angels with him, then he will sit on his glorious throne. Before him will be gathered all the nations, and he will separate them one from another as a shepherd separates the sheep from the goats, and he will place the sheep at his right hand, but the goats at the left. Then the King will say to those at his right hand, "Come, O blessed of my Father, inherit the kingdom prepared for you from the foundation of the world; for I was hungry and you gave me food, I was thirsty and you gave me drink, I was a stranger and you welcomed me, I was naked and you clothed me, I was sick and you visited me, I was in prison and you came to me." Then the righteous will answer him, "Lord, when did we see thee hungry and feed thee, or thirsty and give thee drink? And when did we see thee a stranger and welcome thee, or naked and clothe thee? And when did we see thee sick or in prison and visit thee?" And the King will answer the, "Truly, I say to you, as you did it to one of the least of these my brethren, you did it to me." Then he will say to those at his left hand, "Depart from me, you cursed, into the eternal fire prepared for the devil and his angels; for I was hungry and you gave me no food, I was thirsty and you gave me no drink, I was a stranger and you did not welcome me, naked and you did not clothe me, sick and in prison and you did not visit me." Then they also will answer, "Lord, when did we see thee hungry or thirsty or a stranger or naked or sick or in prison, and did not minister to thee?" Then he will answer them, "Truly, I say to you, as you did it not to one of the least of these, you did it not to me." And they will go away into eternal punishment, but the righteous into eternal life (Matt. 25:31-46).

"Why must we be judged again if we are judged immediately after our death?" asked Johannes.

The answer is that on the last day we shall rise from the dead and the Last Judgment will be after the resurrection of the body. Body and soul will be reunited, and we shall be judged as full men. After the ascension of our Lord, the angel said to the Apostles, "This Jesus, who was taken up from you into heaven, will come in the same way as you saw him go into heaven" (Acts 1:11). "And they will see the Son of man coming on the clouds of heaven with power and great glory" (Matt. 24:30) to "judge the living and the dead."

All of mankind, from Adam and Eve to the very last one, shall be assembled, and the hearts of men shall lie bare for all to see. Tradition says that the Last Judgment will be on earth on the very scene of our Lord's greatest humiliation, between the Garden of Olives and Calvary. From the Scriptures we know that all the angels, the good ones and the evil ones, will be present. "The angels that did not keep their own position but left their proper dwelling have been kept by him in eternal chains in the nether gloom until the judgment of the great day" (Jude 6). All of God's intelligent creation will be there. Christ will sit on His throne, and His Apostles will also sit on 12 thrones to judge.

Then I saw a great white throne and him who sat upon it; from his presence earth and sky fled away, and no place was found for them. And I saw the dead, great and small, standing before the throne, and books were opened. Also another book was opened, which is the book of life. And the dead were judged by what was written in the books, by what they had done. And the sea gave up the dead in it, Death and Hades gave up the dead in them, and all were judged by what they had done. Then Death and Hades were thrown into the lake of fire. This is the second death, the lake of fire; and if any one's name was not found written in the book of life, he was thrown into the lake of fire.

Then I saw a new heaven and a new earth; for the first heaven and the first earth had passed away, and the sea was no more. And I saw the holy city, new Jerusalem, coming down out of heaven from God, prepared as a bride adorned for her husband; and I heard a loud voice from the throne saying, "Behold, the dwelling of God is with men. He will dwell with them, and they shall be his people, and God himself will be with them; he will wipe away every tear from their eyes, and death shall be no more, neither shall there be mourning nor crying nor pain any more, for the former things have passed away" (Rev. 20:11–21:4).

CHAPTER
23

"BEGONE, SATAN!"

The best preparation for a discussion of hell is a meditation on heaven. Hell is the complete absence, and also forever and ever, of everything heaven is. Our Lord said, "I am gentle and lowly in heart" (Matt. 11:29), and "Come to me, all who labor and are heavy laden, and I will give you rest" (Matt. 11:28). This gentle Lord — after whom the multitudes were flocking because of His endless mercy and kindness — mentions hell 37 times in the Gospels. John the Evangelist says at the end of his gospel that if he were to tell all he remembers, the world could not contain all the books. That gives us the right to take what *is* written down as only a kind of "table of contents," and multiply it to our hearts' content. Therefore, He may have talked very much more often about this most serious subject, the place "where their worm does not die, and the fire is not quenched" (Mark 9:48) and where "men will weep and gnash their teeth" (Matt. 8:12).

Hell is a mystery. It is the answer to the *mysterium iniquitatis,* whereby man, with an act of his free will in cool consideration, chooses to do without God. To this, the only logical consequence is hell. Time and again one hears people object to the fact of eternal hell as being unworthy of the kind of Heavenly Father who could not possibly torture His children in this way forever. This is merely sentimental, and only shows that these people have not yet comprehended what it means that we are created with a free will. In complete freedom we choose hell. We are not pushed into it.

It has been said of heaven, that it has not "entered into the heart of man, what things God hath prepared for them that love him" (Isa. 64:4; 1 Cor. 2:9). We have no idea of the wonders God has in store for us. The same thing could be said of hell. It has not entered into human hearts, what is prepared for those who hate Him. Only once did our Lord lift the veil a little bit when He told the story of Lazarus and the rich man (Luke 16:20–31). This rich man was not a criminal in our sense. He was not a murderer or a thief. He didn't do anything especially wrong worth mentioning. But he didn't have charity. Lazarus, at his doorstep, was starving, and he didn't help him. He falls under the following condemnation: "Depart from me, you cursed, into the eternal fire prepared for the devil and his angels. . . . Truly, I say to you, as you did it not to one of the least of these, you did it not to me" (Matt. 25:41–45).

What a terrific warning. One can go to hell not only for what one has done, but also for what one has not done. The next thing we learn is that the rich man can look over into paradise, where Lazarus dwells in Abraham's bosom. How amazing that the damned can perceive the blessed with the unending reproach to themselves: "There I could be now, too." Then the rich man tried to make connections and was told, "Between us and you a great chasm has been fixed, in order that those who would pass from here to you may not be able, and none may cross from there to us." When the rich man pleaded that Lazarus should be allowed to bring a message to his rich brethren, he was told, "They have Moses and the prophets; let them hear them" (Luke 16:23–29). Right there we meet this *mysterium iniquitatis* again: One day our Lord will rise from the dead, and so many throughout the centuries will have chosen not to believe.

Hell was started before the creation of man with that group of angels who did not want to obey. In their infernal hatred and jealousy, they envy every human soul the joys of heaven, which they have voluntarily forsaken. Therefore, they are our archenemies. "Be sober, be watchful," says Peter. "Your adversary the devil prowls around like a roaring lion, seeking some one to devour" (1 Pet. 5:8). In ancient and medieval times Satan and hell were realities. Everybody knew about them, talked about them, and watched against them. More and more, however, Satan and his evil spirits have succeeded in our "age of enlightenment" in vanishing into a realm of myths. What grownup or, as far as that goes, what high school student believes in a personal devil in our days? This incognito has become his strongest weapon. Behind this spiritual smoke screen he is doing untold harm, and he gets away with it unnoticed.

Our Lord himself, when He allowed Satan to tempt Him, gave us an example of how to deal with our greatest enemy and remain victorious: "Begone, Satan!" (Matt. 4:10).

Chapter 24

"No Eye Has Seen"

What began with the harmless question of a little boy, "Can Martina see us now?" became a never-ending pondering of the whole family on life after death. Our initial questions were answered. Yes, Martina can see us if the rich man could see Lazarus. She does remember us and her life among us — if the rich man remembered his brothers and their way of living. As God is omnipresent — everywhere — and the souls of the blessed are in Him, isn't it very likely that they surround their beloved ones on earth, loving them more than ever before? That is why the funeral service of the church is so consoling and uplifting: "O grave, where is thy victory? O death, where is thy sting?" (1 Cor. 15:55).

Also we read, "Come, O blessed of my Father, inherit the kingdom prepared for you from the foundation of the world" (Matt. 25:34). These will be the words addressed on the last day to those who will enjoy the beatific vision from then on, forever and ever. The kingdom of Heaven! That was one of our Lord's favorite topics, and He tried so hard to make us understand what it is like. One day, God willing, we shall find out for ourselves. Meanwhile, we have to believe Paul, who says, "What no eye has seen, nor ear heard, nor the heart of man conceived, what God has prepared for those who love him" (1 Cor. 2:9).

Even if we are warned that it hasn't entered any human heart, we can always begin to try to imagine it. We shall be united with the One "whom our soul loves," and this union will be more intense and more tender than any union between the most loving couple here on earth. Many times we have found out that we cannot love what we do not know. We shall know God as He is. Therefore, we shall love Him to an extent inconceivable to us now. We shall be at rest. We shall be happy. Oh — for the poverty of words! We shall be together with the man of Nazareth, who will recognize us as His disciples if we now patiently bear our daily cross.

"My Lord and my God" (John 20:28), we shall keep on repeating. "Rabboni! I love thee!" If in Galilee five thousand people could follow Him into the desert forgetting time and hunger because they were so fascinated by His personality, what will be in store for us when we shall see Him in His risen glory, the fairest of men, the best of friends, the most humble of all masters, He the changeless one!

We shall be united also with His mother and all His friends in a most intimate friendship. We shall be able to converse with Peter, John, Moses, and other greats of Christianity. We shall find those millions and millions of saints, each mirroring the eternal God in another way. Then there will be the myriad of angels, and our own guardian angel!

And all our friends and relatives, husbands, children, and wives will all be together — together in God! We shall remain the individuals we have been here on earth, but the possibilities which were created into us shall now find fulfillment. And nothing will any more disturb our complete oneness with God. In Him we shall know all other things. In Him we shall meet His other children. Nothing will ever draw our attention away from Him. And all this, forever and ever. "With the Lord one day is as a thousand years, and a thousand years as one day" (2 Pet. 3:8).

Yes, truly, as we read these Holy Scriptures we who know Jesus as our Savior should praise Him and leap for joy at the thought of such a glorious forever. John saw in his vision the glory of heaven and recorded it:

> Then he showed me the river of the water of life, bright as crystal, flowing from the throne of God and of the Lamb through the middle of the street of the city; also, on either side of the river, the tree of life with its twelve kinds of fruit, yielding its fruit each month; and the leaves of the tree were for the healing of the nations. There shall no more be anything accursed, but the throne of God and of the Lamb shall be in it, and his servants shall worship him; they shall see his face, and his name shall be on their foreheads. And night shall be no more; they need no light of lamp or sun, for the Lord God will be their light, and they shall reign for ever and ever (Rev. 22:1–4).

Isn't there something to it? Doesn't it change our perspective? Measured on these giant truths, don't our petty daily troubles shrink into mere insignificance? Let us never forget that we owe it all to Him who "became partaker of our humanity that we might become partakers of His divinity," our changeless friend, Jesus Christ, the same yesterday, today, and yes, forever.

ENDNOTES

Preface

1. Maurice Meschler, *The Life of Our Lord Jesus* (St. Louis, MO: Herder, 1950).

   Francois Mauriac, *Life of Jesus* (New York: David McKay Co., 1951).

Chapter 7

1. Alfred Edersheim, *The Temple: Its Ministry and Services* (Grand Rapids, MI: Wm. B. Eerdmans Publ. Co., 1978).

   Denis O'Shea, *Mary and Joseph, Their Life and Times* (Milwaukee, WI: The Bruce Publishing Co., 1949).

Chapter 9

1. James Hastings, *Dictionary of the Bible* (New York: Scribner, 1963).

Chapter 10

1. Franz M. William, *Mary the Mother of Jesus* (St. Louis, MO: B. Herder Book Co., 1938).

   Denis O'Shea, *The Holy Family* (Dublin: M.H. Gill & Son, Ltd., 1944).

   O'Shea, *Mary and Joseph, Their Life and Times*.

Chapter 11

1. Josephus Flavius, Paul L. Meier, *Josephus: The Essential Writings* (Grand Rapids, MI: Kregel Publications, 1988).

A Word in Between

1. Léonce de Grandmaison, *Jesus Christ* (New York: Sheed & Ward, 1961).

   Marie Joseph LaGrange, *The Gospel of Jesus Christ* (London: Burns, Oates & Washbourne, Ltd., 1938).

Archbishop Alban Goodier, *The Public Life of Our Lord Jesus Christ* (London: Burns, Oates & Washbourne, Ltd., 1936).

Meschler, *The Life of Our Lord Jesus Christ.*

Mauriac, *Life of Jesus.*

Guiseppe Ricciotti, *The Life of Christ* (Milwaukee, WI: Bruce Publishing Co., 1947).

Ferdinand Prat, *Jesus Christ: His Life, His Teaching, and His Work* (Milwaukee, WI: Bruce Publishing Co., 1950).

William, *Mary the Mother of Jesus.*

O'Shea, *Mary and Joseph, Their Life and Times.*

O'Shea, *The Holy Family.*

Chapter 15

1. Alfred Barret, *Mint by Night* (New York: America Press, 1938).

Chapter 21

1. Blot, *In Heaven We Know Our Own* (Benziger).

John Peter Arendzen, *What Becomes of the Dead?* (New York: Sheed & Ward, 1951).

Dr. Robert Klimsch, *Leben die Toten (Do the Dead Live?).*

WHEN THE KING WAS CARPENTER

CONTENTS

FOREWORD

How did this book ever come to be written? So far, all my books have had to do with my family. Well, this one at least began with the family, with one incident, 50 years ago.

Little Martina, aged four, didn't like oatmeal. (As this happened back in Europe, we called it porridge.) She used to spread her helping very thinly all over the plate, hoping to create an "almost finished" impression.

In passing by I looked down at her and said, "Martina, the child Jesus would never have done this."

Quick as a wink, she snapped back, "Did He have to eat porridge for breakfast, Mother?"

And, embarrassed, again I had to answer, "Really, I don't know."

Now came the weighty words, "Why don't you find out?"

Her question stuck in me like a dart from then on. And that is the beginning of this book.

At first I tried the "direct question" method. As we had on our estate a chapel and a residing chaplain, there were many visiting priests coming. From now on I would approach each one wistfully, "Excuse me, Father, but could you tell me what Jesus might have had for breakfast when He was a child?" I was so convinced that they must have learned this in their seminaries.

Their answer invariably was, "I have no idea." (And I had thought that the life of Christ was the main topic of all seminary curricula!)

As my first approach to the solution of my problem did not work out, I thought of something else. If I, for instance, wished to know what kind of breakfast Mozart, Shakespeare, or even Julius Caesar ate, I would look into a well-written biography of these people. Therefore, I went into bookstores and libraries and came home with books on the life of Christ written by many eminent theologians, but neither Meschler nor Mauriac nor Ricciotti seemed the least bit interested in this particular question.

The years passed and we had come to America. For a while there were other things more important to be taken care of. But then my query flared up again when I found books now in English about the time of Christ. I had already begun back in Austria to jot down interesting items I had found in books, and now I found so many more.

Finally, I had compiled quite a collection pertaining to the everyday life of a Jewish family at the time of Christ: what were the mother and father's duties; how a boy grew from babyhood into adolescence in five stages, each with a name; what they were wearing; and finally — eureka! — what they were eating. There was the answer to my $64 question: They didn't have any breakfast! They ate two meals a day: one in the late morning and the other in the late afternoon. With this I could have answered Martina and been done with it.

But there was so much interesting material collected already that I went ahead and finished the book. Then I realized that there would be many people who would read the book and be touched by it, having learned to know Jesus as a fellow citizen, so to speak, or a neighbor from next door. But there will be others who will wonder, *Where did she find all this information?* And those I have to disappoint by merely answering with titles and authors, as much as I still remember. (Some information I found when I went to the Holy Land and came in contact with scholars.)

At the end of the book there will be a reference list. My difficulty is that I cannot say now from which book came which information, but these are the only ones from which I gathered what is now so pleasant for you and me to know.

CHAPTER 1

A HAPPY FAMILY

His earliest memories are the days of Nazareth just after the return from Egypt. He must have been about three years old.

The voice of His mother, "Mary of Nazareth," awakened her family every morning at daylight, calling out, "Blessed be he who loveth His people Israel."

Joseph Ben-David, her husband, whom the child called Father, would answer, "Blessed be He who loveth His people Israel." And that was the way the day started in every Jewish household.

The next thing was to make the beds. Each person slept on a narrow mat, which was rolled up and stood in a corner during the day. Their little house had only one room, which was a bedroom, dining room, and living room all in one.

As they put on their outer garments, Jesus could hear His parents pray. He was too small then to understand the words, but He knew that for everything they did throughout

the day there were special "benedictions" to be recited. By
and by He learned them all. There was one benediction for
waking:

> My Lord, the Spirit which Thou hast given
> me is pure. Thou hast created it and formed it
> into me and preservest it within me, And wilt one
> day take it from me And restore it unto me here-
> after. So long as the Spirit is within me, I will
> give thanks unto Thee, O Lord, my God, sover-
> eign of all works, Lord of all spirits. Blessed art
> Thou, O Lord, our God, King of the universe,
> Who restoreth the Spirits unto their bodies.

Then He heard, "Blessed art Thou, O Lord, our God,
King of the universe, who raiseth up those who are bowed
down."

There was a benediction for getting dressed: "Blessed
art Thou, O Lord, our God, King of the universe, who
clotheth the naked."

There was another benediction as they washed their
face and hands: "Blessed art thou, O Lord, our God, King
of the universe, who removeth sleep from mine eyes and
slumber from mine eyelids."

And putting on their sandals, finally they said together,
"Blessed art Thou, O Lord, our God, King of the universe,
who hast supplied me with every want."

All these prayers Jesus was to learn by heart when He
was a little older; but the first sentence His father taught
Him was the beginning of the solemn morning and evening
prayer, the *Sh'ma*: "Hear, O Israel! The Lord, our God, is
one! You shall love the Lord your God with all your heart
and with all your soul and with all your might."

Every morning at the hour of prayer the father would

draw Him close, and together they turned their faces toward Jerusalem. Only the men were required to say the *Sh'ma* twice a day. Women and children were exempt, but this family prayed everything together. Always Jesus' mother joined in — and for Jesus these were the happiest moments of the day when He could talk to His Father in heaven and turn towards His house. Very soon He had learned the entire morning prayer and could repeat it with His whole heart.

The second part followed:

> And if you will obey my commandments which I command you this day, to love the LORD your God, and to serve him with all your heart and with all your soul, he will give the rain for your land in its season, the early rain and the later rain, that you may gather in your grain and your wine and your oil. And he will give grass in your fields for your cattle, and you shall eat and be full. Take heed lest your heart be deceived, and you turn aside and serve other gods and worship them, and the anger of the LORD be kindled against you, and he shut up the heavens, so that there be no rain, and the land yield no fruit, and you perish quickly off the good land which the LORD gives you.
>
> You shall therefore lay up these words of mine in your heart and in your soul; and you shall bind them as a sign upon your hand, and they shall be as frontlets between your eyes. And you shall teach them to your children, talking of them when you are sitting in your house, and when you are walking by the way, and when you lie down, and when you rise. And you shall write them upon the doorposts of your house and upon your gates,

that your days and the days of your children may be multiplied in the land which the LORD swore to your fathers to give them, as long as the heavens are above the earth. For if you will be careful to do all this commandment which I command you to do, loving the LORD your God, walking in all his ways, and cleaving to him, then the LORD will drive out all these nations before you, and you will dispossess nations greater and mightier than yourselves (Deut. 11:13–23).

In the third part of the morning prayer the family professed openly to be God's people by wearing a special sign on their clothes:

> The LORD said to Moses, "Speak to the people of Israel, and bid them to make tassels on the corners of their garments throughout their generations, and to put upon the tassel of each corner a cord of blue; and it shall be to you a tassel to look upon and remember all the commandments of the LORD, to do them, not to follow after your own heart and your own eyes, which you are inclined to go after wantonly. So you shall remember and do all my commandments, and be holy to your God. I am the LORD your God, who brought you out of the land of Egypt, to be your God: I am the LORD your God" (Num. 15:37–41).

As soon as Jesus could dress himself, blue knotted threads were attached to His garments, as they were to His father's. Mary took great care of these important signs.

After their morning prayer came the recitation of the

"eighteen benedictions" which everyone, even women, children, or slaves, had to say three times a day. Jesus was too young to memorize that long prayer, but He listened — and loved to watch His mother, who never looked more beautiful than when she was talking with God.

Next, both parents began the day's work. Before starting the duties of the day, every Israelite had to wash his hands and pray, "Blessed art Thou, O Lord, our God, King of the universe, who has sanctified us by Thy commandments and enjoined us to wash the hands."

While the carpenter-father walked over to the workshop, which was in a remote corner of the courtyard, Mary would put on her long veil, saying, "Blessed art Thou, O Lord, our God, King of the universe, who crowneth Israel with glory." Then, taking her son by the hand, she would go out into the yard where the water pitcher stood, stopping on the way through the door to lift Him up to the *mezuza* — a little wooden box with a slit, fastened on the right doorpost. In the box was a small scroll of parchment on which were written some of the text of the *Sh'ma*. This scroll was rolled up and on the outside was written the name of God — *Shaddai* — so that it was visible through the slit. Each time an Israelite passed through the door, going or coming, he touched the Holy name with his fingertips. Then he kissed his fingers.

Mary would now take the empty water pitcher and carry it on her head to the well. When Jesus was a little older He, too, had a small pitcher and was allowed to help carry home the water. The woman of the house always supplied it — and a great deal was needed, because many times throughout the day it was prescribed to wash the hands — before a meal, before starting a new piece of work, or when returning from the town. So Mary made several trips back and forth. She emptied the pitcher into a great stone amphora, which stood in their courtyard and held about 20 gallons.

When that was done, she went to the small hearth on which the family meals were cooked. With some glowing coals and thorny brush, she made a fire in the baking oven. Fire had to be struck with flint and tinder, and to have it go out was a real disaster. So a low fire, carefully stoked and watched, was always burning, and it was used to light stoves, lanterns, and torches. People would even borrow fire from a neighboring house and bring back some of the glowing embers in an earthen vessel. Only in utter necessity would one strike a light. But every boy or girl had to learn how to do it, to be ready for any such emergency.

Then they went into the house. The mother took two wooden bowls, one larger than the other — giving her son the smaller one to hold. Next she went to the wall where Joseph had fastened a wooden container. Jesus would watch fascinated as she removed the stopper and let three measures of golden grain run into the bowl. When she had replaced the stopper, they went outside again and sat down cross-legged, one on each side of their little hand mill. This consisted of two large, heavy stones — the lower one fastened to the floor, while the upper one had a funnel in the middle and a handle with which Mary would grind flour. Jesus held His bowl at the side, waiting for the flour to appear. How He loved helping His mother with her daily tasks!

When the flour was ground, Mary mixed water and salt with leaven from the previous day's bread. She kneaded the dough in a wooden trough until it was smooth. Then she covered it with a piece of linen and let it rise. After about an hour, the dough was ready. She took the trough from the baking oven, rolled up her sleeves, took a handful of dough, and threw it back and forth over her left forearm. This made it grow thinner and thinner until it looked like a round pancake, which she put on the hot tiles of the oven. After a minute or so she turned it over, and when it was crisp on both sides, the first loaf of bread was ready. She kept doing this with all of the dough until she had a stack of good-smelling, fresh barley bread.

When all of the bread for the day was baked, it was mid-morning. Mary would carry it into the house and call Joseph for the morning meal. By that time the father had also worked for two hours and with good appetites they all sat down. But first, they poured water over their hands, saying, "Blessed art Thou, O Lord, our God, King of the universe, who bringeth forth bread from the earth."

Mary took a low, many-sided table that her husband had made for her and put it in the middle of the room. On this she set the basket of freshly baked bread, a cruse of water, cheese, and fruit. Now all three gathered around the table, sitting on the floor. Each took one of the bread loaves, perhaps 18 inches in diameter, and almost as thin as a cracker. Bread was never cut, always broken. On holidays there was wine as well as water, and olives or dried figs with the bread. For the son there was always goat's milk, which His mother bought from a street vendor and kept in a skin.

After every meal they said:

Blessed art Thou, O Lord, our God, King of the universe, who feedeth the whole world with Thy goodness, with grace, with loving kindness and tender mercy; Thou givest food to all flesh, for Thy loving kindness endureth forever. Through Thy great goodness food has never failed us. Oh, may it not fail us forever and ever, for Thy great Name's sake, since Thou nourisheth and sustaineth all beings, and doest good unto all, and providest food for all Thy creatures whom Thou has created. Blessed art Thou, O Lord, who givest food unto all.

After the morning meal the father greeted his family with a friendly *Shalom* — "peace be with you" — and went back to his work, while Jesus, like all little boys under six years of age, stayed with His mother.

There was another responsibility for the women: they must provide sufficient fuel without spending any money for it. During the dry season, therefore, Jesus accompanied Mary every day out over the barren hillsides; and together they gathered thistles, thorns, and dried grass — good only for the oven. Later in the summer Mary would take along a basket for the dry manure (caravan, camel dung) of the pastures, best for kindling the fire. If they were fortunate enough to be among the first after passing of a caravan the "camel pies" would be plentiful.

In the spring she showed Jesus how to gather wild herbs for the cooking. In the summer they picked figs and grapes, drying them on the flat roof of the house. In the fall, just before the rainy season, there was the olive harvest, and they collected the ripe olives by shaking the trees and also using sticks. The finest and best oil Mary made in a bronze mortar held between her knees, as she sat on the floor pounding the olives with a pestle. This oil, kept in a special pitcher, was only used for the Sabbath lamp. In addition, there was oil for the cooking, and oil set aside to be used as ointment for wounds. Whenever Joseph hurt himself at his work Mary would pour first wine, then oil into the wound.

In Nazareth there are only two seasons: the dry season and the rainy season. In the dry season the family's living room was really the courtyard. There Mary had a big handloom set up under the trees. She thoroughly enjoyed taking her place before the loom. First she strung it with long warp strings of hemp, cotton, wool, or silk. Then she used a shuttle to inset the horizontal threads, or woof strings, between the warp threads. With a large comb she pushed the woof firmly down. At the beginning of each rainy season the father would take the two big wooden uprights which fastened the loom and move them indoors for the wet winter months.

Jesus loved those hours spent sitting next to His mother, as He watched her weaving, spinning, sewing, or mending their garments. She would tell Him beautiful stories of Adam and Eve in the Garden of Paradise; of Noah and the flood; of Father Abraham who almost sacrificed his only son, Isaac; of Joseph in Egypt; of Moses and the great miracles of God performed to protect His people from the pharoah; of the prophet Isaiah and Queen Esther; and of their own ancestors, Ruth and King David.

Sometimes, too, His mother would sing. She had a beautiful voice and loved the ancient psalms sung by King David and King Solomon. Often she sang, "The Lord is my shepherd, I shall not want," but her favorite song began with the words, "My soul doth magnify the Lord," and always as she sang it her face had a solemn expression. Another psalm, which Mary learned from her kinsman Zacharias, began, "Blessed be the Lord God of Israel because he has visited and wrought the redemption of his people."

Sometimes she chose as a last song one she had heard an old man sing in the temple at Jerusalem: "Lord, now lettest thou thy servant depart in peace, according to thy word."

Mary also told Jesus the story of the three young men in the fiery furnace and taught Him the hymn they had sung: "Blessed art Thou, O Lord, the God of our fathers, and worthy to be praised and glorified forever." This song was a long one with many verses. After each verse Jesus would respond: "And worthy to be praised and glorified forever."

In the evening after the meal, Jesus would repeat to His father the beautiful stories He had learned, and liked to surprise him every day with a new story or a new song. Joseph never said much, but the touch of his hand on the boy's head showed his pleasure.

Late in the afternoon Mary would prepare the main meal which had to be eaten before sunset. Once again, of course, hands were washed before the family sat down, and the father said grace to which mother and son answered "Amen." The meal usually consisted of a stew of rice, beans, or lentils, or sometimes cracked wheat with thick soup or a sauce. Meat was only for feast days, but occasionally there was fish or eggs with the stew. The boy Jesus had His special bowl of milk, and honey for His bread. There were no knives or forks, only broken pieces of bread used as spoons and dipped into the same bowl. Sometimes the wafer-thin crisp bread was used as a plate, held in the left hand, while with the right hand they dished from the big bowl to the bread. Eventually the plate was eaten as well.

During the summer months, meals were taken in the courtyard. In this central place they ate and lived, and even slept through the dry season. Sometimes, when the day was especially hot, the three took their mats to the flat roof, hoping to catch a cool breeze up there. On other housetops they could hear neighbors doing the same thing. Before they went to sleep, however, Joseph once again called them together, and with Jesus next to him, began the evening prayer, the *Sh'ma*. At the end, the father would say, "I bless you in the name of Jahweh," and Mary and Jesus would answer, "The blessing of Jahweh be with you."

Then, after a last *Shalom*, they took off their upper garments, stepped out of their sandals, and lay down, hearts filled with gratitude towards their Father in heaven, who once again had bestowed so many blessings on them during the day.

Theirs was a happy family.

CHAPTER 2

"TAPH"

What did the word "family" mean to the carpenter's son? Not only His father and mother, but His grandparents, all His uncles and aunts, even all cousins, though in their Aramaic tongue there was no word for "cousin." Blood relationship was so strong a bond that people spoke only of "sisters" and "brothers." The welfare of each and the decisions which had to be made by any individual were always regarded as a concern of the whole group.

Joseph's family, returning from Egypt to Mary's native town of Nazareth, had found there a large "family" group. Mary had a stepsister whose name was also Mary, whose first husband, Alpheus, had died leaving her with several daughters and two sons, James and Joseph. When this Mary married Cleophas, a brother of Joseph the carpenter, they too had several daughters, and again two sons, Simon and Jude. For the new arrivals, these, and Mary's cousin Elizabeth, were their closest relatives in the whole big group. Here in Nazareth, Joseph Ben-David settled with his wife and child.

Growing children were watched with loving care through eight different stages of development:

YELED, or new-born babe
YONEQ, nursed by its mother
OLEL, when the child begins to ask for other food
GAMUL, at the age of 3, when definitely weaned
TAPH, a child clinging to its mother
ELEM, at 6, when his father starts teaching the
     boy and sends him to school in the synagogue
NAAR, at 10, "one who shakes himself free"
BACHUR, at 12, when the boy is a "ripened
     one," mature before the Law

While the boy Jesus was still the little *taph* clinging to His mother, the peaceful years passed only too quickly. Small children, girls and boys, all played together in one courtyard or another. They did as all children do the world over — they imitated their elders. The girls played at cooking, and the boys went to the father's workshop. Jesus went to the carpenter's workshop to amuse himself with shavings or leftover pieces lying around on the floor. (There are certain old-fashioned holy cards where we see the boy Jesus playfully putting little pieces of wood into crosses. This was as impossible as if our present-day little ones would play hanging a man on the gallows. The cross was a curse, never a plaything.) The children also loved to play Sabbath, with the girls imitating their mothers in the preparations for the holy day, and finally, lighting the Sabbath lamp. The boys, veiling their heads with any handy piece of cloth, would band together in a little group of "men," face towards

Jerusalem, and recite as many prayers as possible.

They also played at marriage and funerals. For a "wedding," some of the boys would blow on their little pipes, and the others would dance. At "funerals" where they buried little animals and locusts, all had to mourn, when they felt hot from so much running about, they would gather in the cool shade of a tree to play word and riddle games.

For the child Jesus, clinging to His mother, the happiest moments were always those spent in her presence. Peacefully, He followed her around the house, to the well, and up and down the surrounding hills, as she went for firewood. In those years He developed a deep love for His mother. Like other children His age, He watched her closely and tried to imitate her. She was always cheerful, with a ready smile and if He hurt himself He would run to her, let her take Him in her arms, and let her quiet His grief with the deep peace of her presence.

Once a week there would be wash day. For her family, Mary provided a double set of clothing for both winter and summer. Usually on Thursday she soaked the clothes, rubbed them, and hung them up to dry. The linen was always bleached in the sun, and for Joseph's working clothes there was a special mixture of soda and potash in the water. Of all their apparel, only the sandals were bought. Everything else Mary spun and wove herself.

Very soon Jesus noticed that she was not given to talk. While other women lingered at the well with lively chitchat about the news of the day, Mary would be an interested listener but never joined in such gossiping. With a friendly smile she would greet the older ones or return the greeting of the younger, then she would merely fill her pitcher and depart.

The boy Jesus was growing quickly. He needed a new pair of sandals as fast as He outgrew the others, which were then always given to a poor child. He loved to go shopping in the bazaars with His mother on market day. All the stores had their goods displayed outside on the street and arranged on tables. There He could see pottery, or expensive imported articles such as metal lamps from Corinth, and cloth from India, Chinese silks, precious woods, carpets, and jewels. Butchers and bakers displayed their goods. There was also fried fish, Syrian wine, glassware from Egypt, and cheap pottery all on display.

Professional scribes had their booths to write letters for the people. Interpreters were always ready for the many foreigners who traveled through town with their caravans. Doves, pigeons, chickens, geese, and ducks would make a great noise in their cages. Next to them would be a vegetable stand with onions, radishes, lettuce, horseradish, lentils, beans, carrots, and chickpeas for sale. There was also an abundance of fruit: pears, apples, dates, plums, nuts, cherries, lemons, pomegranates, figs, olives, and grapes.

Many coins were used, especially the Roman denarius, which was equal to the Greek *drachma* (about 17 cents). This was the usual day's pay for the laborer. The Syrian *stater* was taken as equivalent to the Jewish *shekel* (about 64 cents). Market prices varied: two pigeons would be about 20 cents, a lamb about 50 cents, a sheep about 5 dollars, and a cow 30 dollars. A slave cost up to 34 dollars, and for 5 dollars one could buy a suit for him. A role of sacred Scriptures, copied by a scribe, was as high as 85 dollars.

In their goings and comings together, Jesus came to know from His mother how very important were the greetings of His people. If two men met, both riding on a beast of burden, they dismounted. One might simply turn to the other or take a few steps towards him. A more solemn manner of greeting was to prostrate oneself, touching the floor with the forehead several times. Royalty was greeted so, or with a deep genuflection. Then again, for a prophet or man of God, one would kneel before him and embrace his knees. Only the greatest hurry or most serious duty would excuse one from bestowing a greeting. Failure to return the salutation was almost a curse. Within the families, children kissed their parents, intimate friends, and close relatives in coming and going. "The Lord be with you," one might say, at which the other would answer, "May the Lord bless you." A longer formula said, "The blessing of the Lord come over you," with the answer, "I bless you in the name of the Lord." Of all the greetings, the shortest and simplest was the single word *Shalom* — "Peace be to you."

And "peace" remained with the house and family of Jesus.

CHAPTER
3

THE DAY OF THE LORD

When He was still very young, Jesus noticed that there was one day in the week on which His mother would double the portion of grain to be ground in the morning, and bake twice as much bread as on other days. That was Friday. It was done in preparation for the Sabbath when she would rest like all the other people in the Holy Land.

The Sabbath was their holy day of rest and worship. In all the homes, therefore, there was eager activity each Friday, with the mothers preparing Sabbath meals ahead of time. By afternoon Mary would have finished with the cooking, storing meals for the next day in a wooden chest near the stove in order to keep them warm. Then she would go over to a larger chest which was very beautifully carved, a masterpiece made by Joseph for his bride. There she kept the Sabbath clothes. Now she would lay them out so that all might be dressed and ready when the Sabbath was announced.

Next, Mary cleaned the house. She had a broom made of special bushy dried twigs, and she would sweep the whole house. When all was swept and everything else was ready, the Sabbath lamp filled with new oil, the clothes hung up and ready to be worn, Mary took what looked like a large rolling pin, knelt down on the floor opposite the door, and started rolling the floor smoothly, erasing all footprints. An earthen floor could not be washed with water, but the rolling gave the room a fresh, almost new look. In all homes all over the land this went on, giving Friday a special air of preparation and expectancy.

Every household had a number of wicker partitions, something like screens, which could be put up to create small cells. Mary would put one up now and go in with her Sabbath clothes. When she came out she always looked beautiful in her bright blue upper garment with the linen showing underneath, and fresh white veil over her head. Then she would dress her son. Invariably, after the benediction for the changing of garments, she said, "Listen for the sound of the trumpet!" Jesus would already be listening. From the top of the synagogue in Nazareth, where a man was watching the sky, three signals were given with the trumpet. With the first, at sunset, those working in the fields would stop and return to their homes. As the first star appeared in the sky, a second signal was given, which meant that all artisans, Joseph among them, and all shopkeepers should stop work. Mary and Jesus knew that soon after the second signal the head of the house would appear. Time was allowed for the men to bathe and change their garments before the final and last signal announced the beginning of the Sabbath.

At the third trumpet all three members of the family were ready at the door. Now Mary led the little procession, going over to the corner where the Sabbath lamp was fastened to the wall. The lighting of the lamp was always a solemn moment, and the way she did it filled Jesus' heart with reverence for the day of the Lord. Then they settled down to their Sabbath meal, as Mary brought dishes out of the chest behind the stove. It was a feast-day meal. While during the week only one dish was served, on the Sabbath Mary had many different things on the table. Some of the vegetables, such as small cucumbers and carrots, were eaten raw. While she usually boiled vegetables in water, for the Sabbath they were stewed in oil. A dish of lentil stew was always wonderful, but on the Sabbath there was even boiled meat, usually mutton, in the stew. Sometimes it was chicken, kid, or a young lamb. There was fresh fruit on the table too — grapes, mulberries, dates, pomegranates, and different sorts of nuts. In winter it would be dried fruit. Dates and pomegranates Mary would buy at the bazaar. Other fruit grew in the courtyard. As there was no sugar, they used honey for sweetening. Mary made little cakes and filled them with a paste of dried raisins, figs, dates, and honey. They called it a "fruit cake."

This was the only day in the week when the family ate after sunset, and afterwards, just sat around and talked. It was the only evening when Joseph was not to be seen at work on some whittling. Usually he was making handles for tools, but on the Sabbath evening everyone rested in the light of the Sabbath lamp. Like an angel of God, the holy day atmosphere had entered the house and taken possession of it. When, after evening prayer, Jesus went to bed, His little heart was full of joy, looking forward to the next morning.

At last the eagerly awaited day dawned. After morning prayer on the Sabbath, there was an ample meal of milk, dried fruit, and butter and honey with bread. Then Jesus walked between mother and father to the synagogue.

The narrow streets were all swept clean and seemed

wider and much neater. The bazaars everywhere were closed. It was all very quiet and solemn.

The synagogue was a larger building than their simple homes. It had an anteroom containing great pitchers of water, where all poured water over their hands. As they entered the synagogue, Mary went to a place reserved for the women behind a wooden grille, while Jesus sat down next to His father. In front of them was a stage-like platform on which stood a reading desk, in front of a great curtain. Jesus knew that behind that curtain were kept sacred scrolls of Holy Scripture. Before the reading desk was a bench on which all the important men of Nazareth sat, facing the people.

When the whole congregation had assembled, the precentor of the synagogue gave a sign to the sexton, who signaled the cantor to begin. All arose, and those in the bench on the platform had to turn around so that everyone would be facing the temple in Jerusalem. Then the whole congregation, in unison, would solemnly recite the *Sh'ma*. Next the precentor, whose head was veiled, offered in the name of all present, not all of the "eighteen benedictions" of weekdays, but only the first three and the last three. After each one all would respond, "Amen." Before the last prayer, however, he would turn to them, lift up his hands, and pronounce the blessing of Aaron:

> The Lord bless you and keep you; the Lord show you His face and have mercy on you. The Lord turn His countenance to you and give you peace.

Then all sat down for the chief part of the service, the reading of the Holy Scriptures from the reading desk. One reading was given from the Prophets and seven from the

Law. Readers were notified beforehand so that they could prepare themselves. Men or boys could be chosen. How Jesus looked forward to the day when He, too, might be included. He looked at the readers, hoping and wishing to stand there one day. The reader from the Prophets could choose to his own liking any passage from any Prophet, but the readers of the Law had no choice. Each one took up where the preceding one left off. Within three years they were supposed to have read the books of the Law once. After the sermon, the congregation was dismissed with a blessing.

Outside the synagogue Joseph and Jesus waited for Mary. On the way home they would sometimes make little detours, watching out, however, never to exceed the two thousand paces allowed for the Sabbath (about five-eighths of a mile).

During the week, when women met at the well or were gathering firewood in the afternoon, Mary might hear that someone was ill. Jesus knew then that there would be a visit to the sick person on the Sabbath. When they had returned from the synagogue and had finished their second meal, Mary would say, "Shall we go and see how so-and-so is feeling today?" She always took Jesus with her on those visits to the sick. Mary had great compassion for anyone who was suffering, and she never came with empty hands. She always had Jesus carry a basket with oil and wine, dried fruit, and some of their fruitcake. Even as a small boy He felt what a great consolation went out from His mother when she bent over the sick person with the greeting, *Shalom.*

What Mary did for the sick, she also did for the poor. Although her home was very simple, with just enough to meet their needs, they had everything necessary and were never destitute. Others were much poorer than they were, and when Mary heard of a case of real poverty and starvation, she always found an extra garment in her chest, and also would spin and weave to produce something extra to give to others.

After the little Sabbath walk, they returned to the synagogue for the afternoon service. There was another Scripture reading, usually continued from the one in the morning, but without the solemn liturgical ceremonies.

Then it was time to go home for the evening meal, which must be finished before the appearance of the evening star which terminated the holy day. Again Mary set the table, either in the courtyard or in the room, and decked it with all the delicacies she had prepared. Again the three gathered around it on the floor and, after saying grace, enjoyed the good meal. If Joseph had not accompanied them on the visit, he spoke during supper of what he had done. Sometimes friends or relatives had come to visit him and discuss the topics of the time: the latest outrages of the Romans, the increased prices because of heavy taxation, the impatient awaiting of the Messiah to come.

Nevertheless the day was always filled with holiness and peace, a day of rest for the greater honor and glory of God.

CHAPTER
4

THE HOUSE OF JAHWEH

The most beautiful hours for Jesus were the quiet evenings of story-telling, when His mother would talk to Him of her years in the temple. Schools for girls did not exist since the rabbis feared that domestic duties would suffer if women spent time in study. Mary, however, coming from one of the highest families in the land, had been eligible to become a temple virgin and to receive the best education from learned rabbis and scribes. The maidens in the temple also learned all a woman's domestic duties. They were taught to cook, wash, spin, weave, embroider, and sing, as well as how to read and write.

Over and over, from the time Jesus was old enough to understand, Mary had described for Him the temple, the one place in which sacrifices could be offered to God, the only house of Jahweh on earth. Closing His eyes, He could picture the tremendous piles of stonework towering high over the city of Jerusalem, with Herod's thousands of builders

241

climbing like tiny ants from stone to stone. He could see the pure gold of the great holy house gleaming and sparkling in the sun, the vast courts, cloisters, and colonnades with their brilliantly colored marbles, the massive gold and silver of the great gates.

With each retelling, Jesus was drawn closer and closer to the Holy City He had not yet seen. Step by step in the story, He and His mother would make the pilgrimage. Together they would pause on Mount Olivet. They followed the winding road down into the valley and across the brook Kidron (Cedron). They set their faces for the last steep climb "up to Jerusalem" — up, up, and then suddenly they had come through the gate and were in the great Court of the Gentiles beneath the mighty columns of the royal porch. From the eastern corner of the wall behind them, they could look down to the bottom of the Kidron Valley, and it was of a steepness to make one giddy. Yet in front of them the house of God, the temple itself, towered loftily over all.

Mary's story always took them next to the Court of the Women, where, as a cloistered maiden, she had gone daily, for the sacred ceremonies of the sacrifice. Eagerly her son made her tell it all over again from the beginning. How during the night the temple gates were closed and the massive keys guarded under a marble slab, while the whole vast enclosure was wrapped in silence and darkness. How long before dawn priests and Levites were busy with preparations for the day's sacrifice, which was always a yearling lamb without blemish, an offering of incense, and 12 loaves. Jesus knew that to be a priest of the temple one must descend from Aaron, but that sons of Levi, the Levites, were also in the temple as helpers. Mary had told Him in the words of the Scriptures, "Then Moses stood in the gate of the camp, and said, 'Who is on the Lord's side? Come to me.' And all the sons of Levi gathered themselves together to him" (Exod. 32:26).

When lots had been cast for the first duties of the day, one priest was sent to the pinnacle of the temple to watch for the dawn. When the temple maidens arose, Mount Olivet in the east was still a silhouette against the gray sky. Together they turned their faces toward the House of Gold and solemnly recited the "eighteen benedictions," which one day Mary was to teach her son:

> O Lord, open Thou my lips and my mouth shall declare thy praise. Blessed art Thou, O Lord, our God and God of our fathers. God of Abraham, God of Isaac, God of Jacob, the great, mighty, and revered God, the most high God who bestoweth loving kindness and possesseth all things, who rememberest the pious deed of the patriarchs and in love wilt bring a Redeemer to their children's children. For Thy name's sake."

Then suddenly from behind the hill across the valley came the first ray of sun, and with the watchman's long, loud, drawn-out hail, "The — morning — shineth!" The answering call rose from below: "Is the sky bright as far as Hebron?"

Now the gray of the sky went quickly, and there were glimpses of white in the green valley. Once again the watchman's voice sounded, "The sky is lit up as far as Hebron!"

Instantly, all silence was shattered. The presiding priest lifted his powerful voice and sent out his command: "Priests, to your duties! Levites, to your chants! Israelites, to your places!"

At this moment the Levites opened the great gates,

everyone took his appointed station, and the faithful began to flock into the outer courts.

The temple maidens watched the sacred ceremonies from behind a latticed gallery in the open Court of the Women. As Mary described it so vividly it seemed to her Son that He, too, was peering through the lattice, past the gigantic eastern gate, to catch a glimpse of the huge altar where the triple fire was blazing and great clouds of incense were rising to the sky. Now the lamb was fetched out and given its last drink of a golden bowl. Ninety-three priests took their places. As the silver trumpets sounded a triple signal, the lamb's throat was cut and the blood caught in gold and silver vessels. They could see the white gowns of the priests turn red with the blood as the lamb was cut, skinned, and offered, and behind it all, the beautiful golden house, Jahweh's abode on earth.

Next there would be a tense moment as the second lot was cast to decide which priest might have the honor of offering incense. There was a deep, waiting silence. Suddenly, a dense column of fragrant smoke came curling out through the windows and rising high into the air above the golden roof of the holy house. All the watching faithful fell prostrate in adoration and prayed to God to bless His people and to send His Holy One within their own days.

"Magnified and sanctified be His great name," were the words of the *Kaddish*, "in the world which He has created according to His will. May He establish His kingdom in your life and during your days, and during the life of the whole household of Israel, even speedily, and in the near time, so be it, Amen."

Meanwhile parts of the lamb had been brought to the altar and arranged in the fire. The drink offering was poured out at the base of the altar and 12 half loaves thrown into the flame. Then, all the priests together, standing on the steps, raised their arms shoulder high and recited together the solemn blessing which had been given to the people in the desert: "The Lord bless you, and keep you: the Lord make His face to shine upon you, and be gracious to you: the Lord lift up His countenance upon you, and give you peace" (Num. 6:24–26).

After the blessing, everyone rose to the singing of the psalm of the day. Choir, stringed instruments, and silver trumpets together made such loud and festive music that it could be heard all over the city. When the last chord had died away, the morning sacrifice was over.

There in the courts of the temple, Mary passed her childhood. Day after day she had listened to the mighty sound of the temple drum, the *magrepha*, and had seen the priests' hands raised in blessing over the prostrate people.

Her son could not hear enough about those years or about the glory and majesty of the house of God on earth. Over and over He listened to her tell of it, waiting most impatiently and eagerly for the time when He would be taken along with His mother and father on the annual pilgrimage to Jerusalem. Each time He begged for the story of her years as a temple virgin, His longing to see the house of the Lord grew, especially when He heard her exclaim in the words of their ancestor, David, "O LORD, I love the habitation of thy house, and the place where thy glory dwells" (Ps. 26:8).

On a visit to Salzburg in 1964, Maria visited *The Sound of Music* film set. Here, she shakes hands with Christopher Plummer (the captain in the movie version). Also seen is Robert Wise, producer and director.

(Photo: Photo Fest)

CHAPTER
5

THE FEAST OF FEASTS

Jesus did not have to wait long for the first family pilgrimage to the Holy City. According to the rabbis' decree, a child might partake in the celebration of the holy *Pasch* as soon as he could eat meat.

So one spring day His cousins began telling Him of the wonderful trip ahead, in which He would share this time. On all sides preparations were being made for the pilgrimage. Men were busy repairing the roads, fixing bridges, and whitewashing the sepulchres along the roadside. In the homes women were getting the clothes ready, and in the synagogues special prayers were added in preparation for the great feast. The children were most expectant, eagerly looking forward to the great treat in store for them. Jesus was too young to ask the full meaning of it all, but His small heart could feel the deep religious and patriotic emotions which were aroused everywhere.

Finally the day of departure arrived. All the people

247

from Nazareth went in a group . . . the better to ward off robbers and wild animals. While most of them walked, families with little children used donkeys. Joseph had a donkey which helped him transport heavy beams from the lumberyard to the places where they were needed for new homes. He had made a little chair, attached to the donkey's saddle, for Jesus.

As Jesus rode, He looked around eagerly. A few of the rich people had camels, and one of the very wealthy ones could afford a chariot. All those on foot had a staff in hand, water skins and food baskets hanging from their shoulders. The people had elected a leader of the pilgrimage, and when everybody was ready, he called out, "Arise ye and let us go up to Zion unto the Lord, our God." Whereupon the cantor of the synagogue would intone, "How lovely are thy tabernacles, O Lord of hosts." And everyone would join in, "My soul longeth and fainteth for the courts of the Lord. My heart and my flesh have rejoiced in the living God."

Nazareth lies about 85 miles north of Jerusalem. It took them four and one-half days to make the pilgrimage. Nights were spent at one of the many inns by the roadside. Such an inn, or *khan* consisted of a large walled-in area. The walls were 15 feet high and were a protection during the night against robbers, lions, wolves, and jackals.

In the middle of the inn grounds, the innkeeper kindled a large fire where the pilgrims could warm themselves before lying down on the sleeping mats which they had brought along, covering themselves with heavy camel's-hair coats. Some of the pilgrims took sacrificial animals along from home, while others would buy them at the temple market. Such an inn was a place teeming with men, women, children, camels, donkeys, cattle, and lambs.

After morning prayers, with faces turned toward the Holy City they were approaching, they ate dried fruit and drank water from their skins. Even on the trip, people had already banded together in groups of families and friends, as the Law prescribed that the *Pasch* should be eaten in groups of not less than 12, not more than 20.

The mothers of the group would avail themselves of the large mills and baking ovens made ready by the innkeeper to bake the daily supply of bread from the grain they had brought from home. Soon after six o'clock they would be on the road again. One stop would be made for the noonday meal consisting of dried fruit, bread, cheese, and water or milk. The evening meal would be cooked in the next *khan* — a stew of lentils or beans with plenty of bread. There was a joyous air about the whole group. Though tired after a long day's march, they were happily tired.

As they walked on, passing through hamlets and small towns, other pilgrims would join them until, on the last day, the road would be covered with an unbroken line of people and animals. It was a long procession. Most of the time the travelers would sing hymns and psalms. On the final stage of the trip, pipers led with their instruments. With each day the enthusiasm of the pilgrims kept mounting.

On the last morning Jesus' cousins kept telling Him that soon now they would see the Holy City. And, as they followed once more around a curve in the road, there it was just as His mother had described it to Him, Jerusalem the beautiful, with its massive walls and many towers, and the glorious temple building surrounding them. The golden house — sparkling in the sun! For a moment all noise stopped. A reverent hush fell over the whole large group, until the instruments started again and everyone joined in the singing of Psalm 122: "I was glad when they said to me, 'Let us go to the house of the Lord. . . . Pray for the peace of Jerusalem: may they prosper who love you.' "

At the city gate, representatives of Jerusalem greeted

the pilgrims. There were rulers and treasures of the temple, harpists and choristers with their instruments who said, "Brethren, men of Nazareth, you are welcome!"

They entered the city by the Garden Gate and went first to the place assigned to them, where they were to spend the seven days of the feast.

Jerusalem was bigger — much bigger — than Mary's description had led Jesus to imagine. Everywhere people were coming and going, and the whole vast enclosure seemed to be alive with animals — lowing oxen and hundreds and hundreds of lambs bleating under the burning sun, while pilgrims bartered and bargained, and moneychangers shouted and counted their coins.

Mary and Joseph looked sad as they hastened by such noisy, dishonest groups. They worked their way across the great courtyard, and around the *sorag*, a low screen of marble pillars, to the eastern side of the inner wall. Mount Olivet and Gethsemane were behind them, as they mounted the 14 steps, crossed a broad platform, and stood before the Beautiful Gate, the main entrance to the temple.

First came the Court of the Women. Up a flight of marble steps flashed the gleaming gold and silver of the Nicanor Gate, beyond which Jesus knew were the great altar of holocausts and the temple itself. Mary remained in the Court of the Women as Joseph and Jesus proceeded up the steps and into the "Court of Israel."

Before them, in the Court of the Priests, stood the great altar of holocausts with its tremendous bulk of unhewn stone, and below it the Brazen Laver, a huge flower-shaped bowl resting on 12 brass bulls. They could see in the marble floor the rings to which sacrificial animals would be tied. On the great silver table, the gold and silver vessels of the sacrifice gleamed in the sun, and on the table of the altar itself, three fires burned steadily.

It was forbidden to enter the temple with sandals, bags, and staff, or dust on one's feet, so their sandals and all traveling equipment were left outside. The leader of the pilgrimage cautioned them that even in front of the gates reverence and respect were to be shown.

In a whisper, Joseph pointed out the entrance to the holy house and the veil of four colors behind which dwelt the living God. Deep joy and holy awe flooded the heart of Jesus.

Jesus had an uncle by the name of Zacharias who was from the tribe of Aaron and was a priest for the temple. He and his wife, Elizabeth, lived in Ain-Karim, only a short distance outside of Jerusalem in the hills, but he had also a house in the city. As long as the old coupled lived, Mary, Joseph, and Jesus were most probably invited to spend the Holy Week with them in Jerusalem. They had only one son, John, whom Jesus had never met. During the stay in their home, He overheard His aunt telling His mother that the young boy had gone away into the wilderness to lead the strict life of a hermit.

Zacharias also invited friends from the nearby village of Bethany. They had three children — a boy, Lazarus and two girls, Martha and Mary. They were usually members of the group celebrating the *Pasch* together.

The Passover was always held on the same day, the 14th of the month Nisan (April). On the preceding evening everyone met in the dining room. Then Uncle Zacharias, head of the house, appeared with a lighted candle, and as all faced toward the temple, he prayed, "Blessed art Thou, Jahweh, our God, King of the universe, who hast sanctified us by Thy commandments and commanded us to remove the leaven."

Next he searched by candlelight into every corner of the room, especially in all places where leaven was usually kept. Of course, the women had removed it all earlier. This was only a ceremonious search, after which he prayed again: "All the leaven that is in my possession, that which I have seen and that which I have not seen, be it null, be it counted as the dust of the earth."

This search was accomplished in perfect silence. For seven days the only bread to be used was unleavened loaves. The boy Jesus was deeply touched by the search for the leaven.

The feast for which they all had come to Jerusalem was really threefold: the *Pasch*, the Feast of the Unleavened Bread, and the Feast of the First Fruit.

The next day, the 14th of Nisan, was the holiest day of the seven. From noon on, no work was done; the whole city took on a festive air.

Early in the morning the fathers, who were responsible for the eating of the paschal lamb, went out to select the proper animal, one without blemish, not more than one year, not less than eight days, old.

During their first few Passovers Joseph went alone for the paschal lamb, slaughtered it in the temple, offered its blood, had it skinned and brought it to His uncle's home, while Jesus stayed with His mother who helped His aunt with the preparations for the solemn meal at night.

His uncle was saddened that people of his time were beginning to forget many of the old customs. He, himself, was very strict. In the entrance hall to the dining room he kept special mantles, staffs and wide-brimmed hats ready for all participants; and, as each entered the room, he was handed his set by a servant. Then all stood around the long table with Zacharias presiding, and they were told to eat and drink in haste according to the word of Moses: "In this manner you shall eat it: your loins girded, your sandals on your feet, and your staff in your hand; and you shall eat it in haste. It is the LORD's passover" (Exod. 12:11).

One of the exciting things of this night for small children was that they were allowed to stay up long beyond their usual time. The solemn meal started around nine o'clock in the evening. It began with a cup of wine mixed with water. Then all washed their right hands again, took some of the lettuce, dipped it in a tart sauce, and ate it.

Next Zacharias pronounced solemnly the blessing over the lamb: "Blessed is He who sanctifies us with His commandments and ordered us to eat the Passover."

The paschal lamb was brought in, and the bitter herbs were dipped and eaten together with the meat of the lamb. Next the second cup of wine was served. That was the moment when everyone looked at the son of Mary and Joseph. He was the youngest first-born boy at the table, and as such had the right to ask the question of the evening: "Why is this night different from other nights? For on all other nights we eat leavened bread, but on this night only unleavened bread? On all other nights we eat any kind of herbs, but on this night only bitter herbs? On all other nights we eat meat stewed or boiled, but on this night only roasted? On all other nights we dip the herbs only once, but on this night twice?"

Jesus had been memorizing this long question weeks ahead of time, and now He was happy when He could see in the eyes of His mother and father that He had said it well.

In answer to the question, Zacharias instructed them all while addressing himself to the boy about the importance of the night. He began with their people's disgrace in Egypt, ending with their future glory. He gave a learned discourse about their whole national history and explained each small detail. Then more cups of wine were served, four in all, each preceded by another washing of hands, and during all that time the great "*Hallel* Psalms" were sung by the family group. After one last benediction, the father of the house dismissed them. In the anteroom they took off their liturgical garments, and in solemn silence everyone withdrew to go to sleep. High in the sky the big bright moon, the full moon of spring, shed its light on this holy night.

The next day, the 15th of Nisan, was called "the first day of the unleavened bread." It was still a holiday with no unnecessary work done, and all went to the morning sacrifice and to the temple. After the public sacrifice for the whole nation was offered, the private offerings of each individual were brought. On the next day was the Feast of the First Fruit. In the evening (all days started in the evening, instead of morning) just as the sun went down, three men, each with a sickle and basket, went to a place which was marked out by the elders where the new barley was to be cut. A whole procession went with these men and they asked of the bystanders four questions:

"Has the sun gone down?"
The people would answer, "Yes."
"Should we reap with this sickle?"
The people answering, "Yes."
"Into this basket?"
"Yes."
And finally, "Shall I reap?"
The people again responded: "Thou shalt
reap."

They then cut down ceremoniously a bushel of the new barley. The ears were brought into the court of the temple to be threshed with flails, then parched on a perforated pan over the hold fire, and exposed for the wind. The grain thus prepared was ground in a barley mill. The flour was passed through many sieves, each one finer than the other, until it was fine enough to be offered in the temple. Mixed with oil and frankincense, it was waved before the Lord. A handful was taken out and burned before the altar; the remainder belonged to the priests. That was called the "Presentation of the First Fruit," on the second day of the Passover Feast on the 16th of Nisan.

The next days were minor feast days. All work was allowed again. The last day of the Passover, the 21st of Nisan, was a great holiday again and observed like a Sabbath.

Year after year Jesus came to Jerusalem with His mother and father, fulfilling the duty imposed on Him by the ancient Law and customs of His people. Each year He understood more of the holy ceremony and penetrated more deeply into the liturgical meaning of this memorial feast of the redemption of Israel.

As a little boy He had greatly enjoyed spending part of the day roaming around with cousins and friends through the fabulous bazaars of Jerusalem, but as He grew older, He no longer felt drawn to these childish pastimes. He wanted to "dwell in the courts of the Lord," as had His ancestor David.

More and more, too, He saw that their Feast of the Passover had a twofold meaning. It was a memorial of the great things God had done for His people in the past, but it was also a symbol of things to come when, in a much greater Passover than the ones they were then celebrating, He would redeem His people from their sins.

CHAPTER
6

THE SON OF JOSEPH THE CARPENTER

When Joseph Ben-David began to teach Jesus the entire *Sh'ma* and the Psalms of the *Hallel* (Ps. 112-117), Jesus stopped being a *taph*. He was now an *elem*, and shortly after His sixth year, with other boys of His age, began to go to school. There was an elementary school attached to every synagogue, and from the age of five, boys were sent there to learn the Law and to read the *Torah*, the five books of Moses, known as the *Pentateuch*.

Such schools were very austere. The morning session began at six and lasted for four hours in the summer, a little longer in winter. Jesus went home for the morning meal, as did the others. In the afternoon, all returned to school and stayed until supper, though on feast days and fast days the hours were somewhat shorter.

The boys wore tunics and cloaks, the older ones also having a covering for their heads. At all times they sat on the floor in a respectful group with their teacher. Each brought with him a wax tablet, a stylus, and a small parchment roll of the Law. Moses had said, "These words, which I command you this day, shall be upon your heart, and you shall teach them diligently to your children" (Deut. 6:6–7). This was taken literally. It was the custom to begin with the Book of Leviticus, then follow with the other four books and, after that, the Prophets and other sacred writings.

Besides learning to read Hebrew, the boys were also instructed in the meaning of the holy texts. All their knowledge and wisdom came from the Scriptures, which also served as textbooks for history, geography, and philosophy.

Once the boys had started going to school they separated from the girls and played alone in their free time. They would climb the hills behind Nazareth, and loved to watch vine dressers in the vineyards at the time of harvest, or the sowers scattering seed in the early rainy season. They saw the grain winnowed and harvested, and during the threshing they followed the oxen round and round their turning circle.

While the boy Jesus, now an *elem*, still helped His mother carry water and collect firewood, the free hours when He had watched her weaving or spinning were now spent in another way. He was in Joseph's workshop, becoming an apprentice.

This apprenticeship would last for ten years. At first the father merely showed Him how to hold tools, how to plane, how to use a chisel, and to wedge two boards. School took most of the morning and afternoon hours, so what He learned in Joseph's workshop was usually by watching.

As He watched, His admiration, love, and respect grew steadily for the young man who was such a loving father. Joseph, the carpenter, was truly of royal blood. His grave dignity of speech and manner impressed all the neighbors, who were well aware of exalted birth and, when availing themselves of his services as carpenter would respectfully address him by his title — Joseph Ben-David — Joseph, son of David.

He was also a skilled artisan and an independent tradesman, a combination of cabinetmaker, carpenter, and builder, a "just man" who worked zealously so that his wife and son might suffer no want. The work of a carpenter was always in demand, especially since King Herod kept 15,000 men at work on the temple in Jerusalem and had drained the countryside of nearly all skilled labor. Young and capable craftsmen like Joseph, who did not want to work for Herod, were much sought-after and had always more business than they could handle.

Theirs was a quiet house. If Mary was not given to many words, Joseph was still more silent. As Joseph and Jesus worked side by side in the shop or courtyard, time would pass without a word. Joseph would beckon when he wanted to show something to his son. He would nod if the boy worked well, or smilingly shake his head and show him again. He would always listen gravely to the talkative neighbors, saying what he wanted to say in very few words. Only when he explained the Law to Jesus would he become eloquent. His eyes shone and his youthful face glowed with an inner light when he talked about the mercy of God toward his people.

Joseph had only one wish: to purchase all of the holy books. These hand-copied scrolls were very expensive, but patiently he added coin to coin until he could afford yet another. Then he would come home from the market, showing happily his newest treasure and reading to his family in the evenings, or on the Sabbath.

He would read about their ancestors, the illustrious Kings David, Solomon, Hezekiah, and Josiah; or the wicked ones, Uzziah and Manasseh; famous men like Boaz and

Zerubbabel; or women of such diverse fame as Rahab, Ruth, and Bathsheba.

The humble Joseph was nevertheless glad to point out that he and his wife were both of royal blood. He would explain to Jesus that the most famous rabbi of their time, Hillel, who was also descended from David, was nevertheless of inferior birth because his lineage went back, not through the kings to Solomon, the son of David and Bathsheba, but to Abigail, the mischosen wife of David, who was not the mother of any of his royal successors.

Up to His 12th year Jesus was called "son of Joseph," but His father always pointed out that when He became of age He would inherit His official title of royalty and from then on be called "Jesus, son of David."

The family of David was respected as the first family in the land because all people knew that someday the Messiah was to be born from among them.

Chapter 7

"Praising the Lord with Cymbals"

Three times a year the Jewish people were required to go to the Holy Place in Jerusalem. (Those who were more than a day's journey away were not strictly obliged.) God had sent word through the lawgiver, Moses, that at certain intervals they should pause to lift up their hearts and minds to God and to commemorate the great things He had done for them.

On the 15th of Nisan, God gathered His people around the sanctuary for the solemn Feast of *Pasch*. This time they were to come with grateful heart and recall how He had helped them against their mighty enemy, the pharaoh of Egypt, and had led out His beloved people from captivity into the freedom of the Children of God.

During the Feast of Weeks, or Pentecost, the anniversary of the giving of the Law on Mount Sinai was celebrated.

Once more God called His children to the most joyous of the festive seasons in all Israel, the Feast of Tabernacles. It fell at the time of the year when the hearts of the people were naturally full of gratefulness and gladness, late in the fall, when all of the crops had been stored, all the fruits had been harvested, and the land was expecting the refreshment of the rains to prepare it for a new crop.

These were the three major feasts given to the chosen people by Moses 1,400 years before the time of Jesus. Each feast lasted for a week, and every man was to come to Jerusalem for these times, if he could possibly do so.

Besides these great feasts, there were a number of smaller festivals like the Feast of Purim, celebrating the events told in the Book of Esther, when the Jews were delivered from the Persians. This occurred in the month Adar (March) on the 14th day.

The Feast of Lights — Hanukah — was observed on the 25th of the month of Chislev (a pious tradition makes it December 25), and was instituted by the great countrymen of Jesus, the Maccabees, to commemorate the restoration of worship at the temple after it had been desecrated by the Gentiles. The first new grapes of the year were eaten at this festival.

The "Day of Atonement," *Yom Kippur*, often called simply the "Day of Days," falls on the tenth day of the month (October). That included a most touching ceremony in which the high priest sent the scapegoat away into the wilderness, laden with the people's sins.

Every week had its feast day on the Sabbath, so every month had its festive season on the "day of the new moon," which marked the beginning of each new month. Special priests were on duty to watch for the showing of the new moon, and would announce it to the nation by blowing silver trumpets from the pinnacle of the temple. Instantly, fires would be lit on the Mount of Olives and observed from the neighboring hills. In no time the news spread throughout the country. The words of the priest, "It is sanctified," were intended to give a hallowed character to each month. This was always a very popular feast.

Quite distinct from the other new moons, and more sacred, was that of the seventh month, or "Tishri," as it was called, which marked the commencement of the civil year — New Year's Day. This was known as the "Day of Blowing" because on that day the trumpets were blown all day long in Jerusalem. The new moon of the seventh month was to be observed as a Sabbath day and special offerings were ordained for it.

With the liturgical year and the civil year, there were also two New Year's Days. Besides the civil New Year's Day, all celebrated a liturgical New Year's Day, which was on the first day of Elul (the sixth month). All flocks and herds were tithed, and the rabbis said that all the children of men passed before Jahweh like lambs on this day, as it is written, "He fashioneth their hearts alike, He considereth all their works" (Ps. 33:15).

The ordinary happenings of family life were also elevated and given a festive character. Birth, marriage, and death are the great occurrences in every family the world over. But they did not simply "occur" for the people of Israel; they were celebrated as major feasts with an eight-day celebration, like the major feasts of the Lord.

When a baby was born into a Jewish home, all the children of the neighborhood rejoiced because they knew that a week after the birthday would be the feast of name-giving. If it were a boy, it would be circumcision; if it were a girl, it would be a slightly less solemn ritual. But in either case, all the children of the neighborhood were invited by the parents, who showed the new baby to the children and gave a children's party with cakes, drinks, and games. How many times as a little boy Jesus was invited to such joyful parties in Nazareth!

The greatest event in a family, however, was a marriage feast. Mary was frequently asked to come and take part in the preparations of the different marriages of their large family. The women would start two weeks before with baking and roasting, smoking fish and meat, ordering and arranging. The bridegroom would appoint his best friend to distribute the invitations.

A year before the wedding feast they would have already celebrated the feast of betrothal which took place before two witnesses, where they exchanged a ring. The rabbi asked them certain questions and gave them his blessing. After this betrothal, the two persons were regarded as belonging to each other, almost as if they were already married. In that year the bride worked busily on her dowry.

Then came the great day. On the evening of the wedding feast the bridegroom would come with all his friends to take his bride home. Such a wedding procession could be heard throughout the whole town, there was so much shouting, singing, and flute-playing going on. All the people in the bridegroom's party carried torches, while the bride and bridesmaids were waiting with lighted lamps in their hands. The moment of marriage took place when the bridegroom guided his bride over the threshold of her new home. That made her his wife. Afterwards, the solemn marriage meal took place. The newlywed pair sat under a canopy on a kind of throne in special fine clothing. The meal was always lavish.

Mary told her son how people went into heavy debt to make that day the greatest of their lives. When Jesus used to accompany Mary to the well to help her draw the daily supply of water, He could hear the women chatter for weeks after a wedding about the crown of the bride, her jewels, and her bridal garment.

Even a funeral had its festive character. There always had to be witnesses around a dying person. As soon as the spirit had left the body, the eyes and mouth of the corpse were closed by the nearest of kin. The body was then washed, anointed, and clothed in a white garment. Then it was laid out and the near relatives started to lament loudly. Finally, the professional wailers arrived. They tore their hair; sometimes they even lacerated their cheeks, rent their clothes, cast ashes upon their heads and shrieked loud lamentations.

The burial had to take place within 24 hours. The corpse was bound up for the grave and a special piece of linen was spread over the face. Then the body was placed upon a simple bier and was buried either in the ground or in a cave. In the latter case, a heavy stone was needed to close the entrance against wild animals. For several weeks afterward relatives would wear clothes of mourning.

Besides the celebration of all these feasts, the people of Israel observed a great many folk customs and traditions handed down from generation to generation. Like every other Jewish child, Jesus learned to know them. He was told, for instance, that bread must never be cut with a knife, that it might only be broken. Though friends in other parts of the world went arm in arm, Jesus' people went hand in hand. If a dear friend took his leave to go on a journey, they would drink the cup of friendship on the eve of his departure. It was a little informal gathering of all the friends who broke bread and drank wine as a sign of friendship with the one who was about to depart, as a token that they would never forget each other.

People from towns which were farther than one day's journey away from Jerusalem were not strictly obliged to attend the major feasts at the temple. They could celebrate in their local synagogue. This would have been the case for Joseph and his family, as it took them over four days to get to the Holy City. To miss nine work days is something to consider for every artisan, but Joseph always thought that God cannot be outdone in generosity — that God would make up in His own good way the time one lost on these pilgrimages three times a year.

As soon as Jesus was grown up, He accompanied Joseph and His mother not only for the Passover, but also for the Feast of Pentecost and Tabernacles.

Jesus noticed that the attendance at the temple for the other two feasts was not quite as large as at the Passover, yet the temple area was always crowded. Pentecost began on the evening of the 50th day after Passover. During the first watch (between nine o'clock and midnight) the great altar of holocausts was cleansed and, immediately after midnight, the temple gates were thrown open. Before the morning sacrifice, all the offerings which the people brought to the temple had to be examined by the priests. For that reason they must all be on duty. Each was kept very busy.

The particular offering of the day was that of the two whey-loaves with their accompanying sacrifices of seven lambs, one young bullock, and two rams. In contrast to those of the Feast of Passover, such loaves were made with leaven. Especially fine wheat flour was used and they were baked in the temple the night before the feast. Each loaf had to be four hands wide, seven hands long, and four fingers high — and made about five pounds of bread. These loaves represented the ordinary food of the people and were offered in thanksgiving of the daily bread. As at Passover, the first and seventh days of the Feast of Pentecost were kept as Sabbath, and the days in between were minor feast days.

The festival that all liked most, however, was the Feast of Tabernacles. Somehow everyone was naturally in a most festive mood with the harvest over and all the work done and the expectations for the early rains. This feast the Jewish people celebrated not in their houses, but in little huts which they made from fresh boughs of trees. There they ate, prayed, studied, and slept for a whole week. This practice had been ordained by Jahweh to recall that once His chosen people lived in tents for 40 years, while He kept them waiting in the desert.

Families vied with each other to have the nicest hut. There were special regulations: the huts must be high enough, yet not too high — at least 10 hands, but not more than 30 hands; three of the walls must be made of boughs; they must be fairly covered, yet had to admit sunshine.

In the temple there were special offerings. Again, as at the Passover and at Pentecost, the altar was cleansed during the first night watch and the gates of the temple were thrown open immediately after midnight, when the offerings of the faithful were inspected. Just before the morning service began, a priest, accompanied by a joyous procession with music, went down to the Pool of Siloam where he blew a small amount of water into a golden pitcher. While one procession went for the water of Siloam, another brought willow branches from the Valley of Kidron. These were secured on either side of the altar during the blast of the priests' trumpets, and were then bent over the altar to form a kind of canopy.

The ordinary morning sacrifice proceeded. The priest who had gone with his procession to Siloam had to time his return for the exact moment when his brethren carried up the pieces of the sacrificial animals to lay them on the altar. As the procession entered by the Water Gate, which derives its name from this ceremony, they were received by a threefold blast from silver trumpets. The priest went up to the altar with the water and turned to the left. There he found two silver basins with narrow holes. Into these the wine of the drink offering was poured and, at the same time, the water from Siloam. At the moment when wine and water were being poured out, the temple music began, the singing and playing of the great "*Hallel* Psalms." When the choir came to the words, "O, give thanks to the Lord," all worshipers waved their branches toward the altar, in accordance with the words of the Prophet, "With joy you will draw water from the wells of salvation" (Isa. 12:3). With these ceremonies prayers were offered for the much-needed rains.

Every day, at the end of the morning sacrifice, the priests formed a procession and made the circuit of the altar, singing, "Oh, then, now work salvation, Jahweh. O, Jahweh, give prosperity."

And on the last day of the feast, the so-called "Great Day," they made a circuit of the altar seven times, remembering how the walls of Jericho had fallen, and praying that similarly the walls of paganism would fall before Jahweh.

These were most joyful days, the "Day of the Great Hosannah," the "Day of the Great Willows," the "Day of the Beating of the Branches," and finally, the "Great Day."

There was one more ceremony connected with this feast, one which made it especially popular. At the close of the first day the worshipers went to the Court of the Women where great preparations had been made. When they were soiled, the vestments of the priests could not be washed and used again, so they were torn up and made into wicks for lamps. Then four golden candelabras were prepared, each with four golden bowls. Four young priests filled each bowl with the finest oil and lit the wicks with holy fire from the altar. All the faithful had come with torches or lamps in their hands and received the holy fire, which they carried home with them. There was not one court in Jerusalem that was not lit up with holy light, and the whole temple was illuminated, as a sign that the people "who walked in darkness have seen a great light" (Isa. 9:2).

On the afternoon of the seventh day the great celebration was over and the people began to move from their huts back into their homes.

Not for anything would Jesus have missed this feast. Again and again He was deeply moved by the ceremonies of the living water and the holy light.

Maria among her favorite things —
flowers and mountains.

CHAPTER
8

THE SON OF DAVID
THE KING

F inally came the day to which each boy of Jesus' age looked forward with most eager longing: the 12th birthday when he would be declared a "son of the Law."

This was and still is a great day in every Jewish family, known as *Bar Mitzvah.* On the evening of the feast the father would give to his son, together with a solemn blessing, the phylacteries which, from now on, he would be obliged to wear during prayer time, one small box to be fastened around the forehead, and another around the left upper arm. These little boxes contained strips of parchment on which passages of Holy Scripture were written. Then he would give him the *talith,* a beautifully woven shawl to be worn over the head during prayer at home, in the synagogue, and in the temple.

When a boy was initiated into the Law on his 12th birthday, he had to recite the phylacteries and also from then on, three times a day, the *Shemoneh Esreh,* the "eighteen benedictions," the prayers:

1. Be thou praised, O Lord, our God, the God of our fathers, the God of Abraham, of Isaac and Jacob, the great and mighty and dreadful God, the Supreme Being, dispenser of benefits and of favors, the Creator of all things, Thou rememberest the piety of the patriarchs, and Thou wilt send a deliverer to their children, to glorify Thy name and to show forth Thy love. O King, our help, our strength and shield; be thou praised, O Lord, the shield of Abraham.

2. Thou art mighty forever, O Lord. Thou causest the wind to blow and the rain to descend. Thou sustainest the living, thou quickenest the dead. Blessed art Thou, O Lord, that quickenest the dead.

3. Thou art Holy and holy is Thy name. And holy ones praise Thee every day. Praised be Thou, O Lord, the holy God.

4. Thou givest man wisdom and fillest him with understanding. Praised be Thou, O Lord, the dispenser of wisdom.

5. Bring us back to Thy law, O our Father; Bring us back, O King, into Thy service; Bring us back to Thee by true repentance. Praised be Thou, O Lord, who dost accept our repentance.

6. Pardon us, O our Father, for we have sinned. Pardon us, O our King, for we have transgressed. Thou art a God who dost pardon and

forgive. Praised be Thou, O Lord, who dost pardon many times and forever.

7. Look upon our misery, O Lord, and be Thou our defender. Deliver us speedily for Thy glory for Thou art the Almighty Redeemer. Blessed art Thou, O Lord, the Redeemer of Israel.

8. Heal us, O Lord, and we shall be healed; Help us and we shall be helped. Thou art the One whom we praise. Vouchsafe healing to all our wounds, Thou art the King Almighty, our true physician full of mercy! Blessed art Thou, O Lord, who healeth the sick of the children of Thy people.

9. Bless us, O Lord, and bless this year and these harvests. Give Thy blessing to the ground and satisfy us with Thy goodness, and make this year one of the good years. Blessed art Thou, O Lord, who blesseth the years.

10. Sound the trumpet of deliverance; lift the standard which shall gather together the dispersed of the nation, and bring us all quickly back again from the ends of the earth. Blessed art Thou, O Lord, who gathereth Israel.

11. Restore our judges as in former times and our counselors as in the beginning, deliver us from affliction and anguish. Do Thou alone reign over us by Thy grace and mercy, and let not Thy judgment come upon us. Blessed art Thou, O Lord, who loveth truth and uprightness.

12. And for slanderers let there be no hope. Let all workers of iniquity and the rebellious be destroyed; let the might of the proud be humbled.

Blessed art Thou, O Lord, that humblest the arrogant.

13. Let Thy mercy, O Lord, be showed upon the upright, upon the humble, the elders of Thy people Israel, and the rest of its teachers; be favorable to the pious strangers among us and to us all. Give Thou a good reward to those who sincerely trust in Thy name, that our lot may be cast among them in the world to come; that our hope be not deceived. Blessed art Thou, O Lord, the trust of the righteous.

14. Return Thou in Thy mercy to Thy city Jerusalem. Make it Thine abode as Thou hast promised, let it be built again in our days. Let it never be destroyed! Restore Thou speedily the throne of David. Blessed art Thou, O Lord, who buildest Jerusalem.

15. Do Thou cause the branch of David speedily to flourish, and make it glorious by Thy strength for in Thee do we hope all the day. Blessed be Thou, O Lord, who dost make *all things* glorious.

16. Hear our voice, O Lord, our God, and have mercy upon us. Hear our prayers in Thy mercy and loving kindness; for Thou art the God that hearest prayer and supplication. Send us not away, O our King, until Thou hast heard us. Thou dost graciously receive the prayers of Thy people Israel. Praised be Thou, O Lord, who hearest prayer.

17. Accept, O Lord, our God, Thy people Israel, restore Thou the service in the courts of Thy

house. May our eyes see the day when Thou in Thy mercy wilt return to Zion. Praised be Thou, O Lord, who wilt establish Thy dwelling place in Zion.

18. We confess that Thou art the Lord, our God, and the God of our fathers for ever and ever. Thou art the rock of our life, the shield of our salvation from generation to generation. Blessing and praise be unto Thy great and Holy name, For the life which Thou hast given us; for our souls which Thou dost sustain; for the daily miracles which Thou dost work in our behalf; for the marvelous, loving kindness with which thou dost surround us at all times — In the morning, at mid-day and in the evening. God of all goodness, thy mercy is infinite; Thy faithfulness fails not — we hope in Thee forever. For all these Thy benefits Thy name be praised forever and ever. Let all that live praise Thee. Let them praise Thy name in sincerity. Praised be Thou, O Lord, Thy name alone is good, and Thou alone art worthy to be praised. Give peace and blessing unto us even unto Israel Thy people. Bless us all together, O Lord our God. Blessed art Thou, Lord, that blessest with peace. Amen.

It was a great and solemn moment when, on the eve of Jesus' 12th birthday, His father helped Him to put on the phylacteries. His mother had made the little cases from the hide of a black calf. The leather strip she had sewn on had a loop through which passed a thong, one finger wide and 24 inches long. This was the case for the arm and it contained one rolled strip of parchment on which the following text was written:

1. The LORD said to Moses, "Consecrate to me all the first-born; whatever is the first to open the womb among the people of Israel, both of man and of beast, is mine." And Moses said to the people, "Remember this day, in which you came out from Egypt, out of the house of bondage, for by strength of hand the LORD brought you out from this place; no leavened bread shall be eaten. This day you are to go forth, in the month of Abib. And when the LORD brings you into the land of the Canaanites, the Hittites, the Amorites, the Hivites, and the Jebusites, which he swore to your fathers to give you, a land flowing with milk and honey, you shall keep this service in this month. Seven days you shall eat unleavened bread, and on the seventh day there shall be a feast to the LORD. Unleavened bread shall be eaten for seven days; no leavened bread shall be seen with you, and no leaven shall be seen with you in all your territory. And you shall tell your son on that day, 'It is because of what the LORD did for me when I came out of Egypt.' And it shall be to you as a sign on your hand and as a memorial between your eyes, that the law of the LORD may be in your mouth; for with a strong hand the LORD has brought you out of Egypt. You shall therefore keep this ordinance at its appointed time from year to year" (Exod. 13:1–10).

2. "And when the LORD brings you into the land of the Canaanites, as he swore to you and your fathers, and shall give it to you, you shall set apart to the LORD all that first opens

the womb. All the firstlings of your cattle that are males shall be the LORD's. Every firstling of an ass you shall redeem with a lamb, or if you will not redeem it you shall break its neck. Every first-born of man among your sons you shall redeem. And when in time to come your son asks you, 'What does this mean?' you shall say to him, 'By strength of hand the LORD brought us out of Egypt, from the house of bondage. For when Pharaoh stubbornly refused to let us go, the LORD slew all the first-born in the land of Egypt, both the first-born of man and the first-born of cattle. Therefore I sacrifice to the LORD all the males that first open the womb; but all the first-born of my sons I redeem.' It shall be as a mark on your hand or frontlets between your eyes; for by a strong hand the LORD brought us out of Egypt" (Exod. 13:11–16).

3. "Hear, O Israel: The LORD our God is one LORD; and you shall love the LORD your God with all your heart, and with all your soul, and with all your might. And these words which I command you this day shall be upon your heart; and you shall teach them diligently to your children, and shall talk of them when you sit in your house, and when you walk by the way, and when you lie down, and when you rise. And you shall bind them as a sign upon your hand, and they shall be as frontlets between your eyes. And you shall write them on the doorposts of your house and on your gates" (Deut. 6:4–9).

4. "And if you will obey my commandments which I command you this day, to love the LORD

your God, and to serve him with all your heart and with all your soul, he will give the rain for your land in its season, the early rain and the later rain, that you may gather in your grain and your wine and your oil. And he will give grass in your fields for your cattle, and you shall eat and be full. Take heed lest your heart be deceived, and you turn aside and serve other gods and worship them, and the anger of the LORD be kindled against you, and he shut up the heavens, so that there be no rain, and the land yield no fruit, and you perish quickly off the good land which the LORD gives you.

"You shall therefore lay up these words of mine in your heart and in your soul; and you shall bind them as a sign upon your hand, and they shall be as frontlets between your eyes. And you shall teach them to your children, talking of them when you are sitting in your house, and when you are walking by the way, and when you lie down, and when you rise. And you shall write them upon the doorposts of your house and upon your gates, that your days and the days of your children may be multiplied in the land which the LORD swore to your fathers to give them, as long as the heavens are above the earth" (Deut. 11:13–21).

As Jesus recited these texts, Joseph secured the arm case, which was placed above the bend of the left arm, where it would press against the heart, giving effect to the commandment, "And these words, which I command thee this day, shall be in thy heart." Then Joseph made a knot out of the thongs in the shape of the letter *yodh*; the rest he wound around the boy's arm until it ended at His middle finger.

The case for the head was made of cowhide. It had four compartments containing separate pieces of parchment on which the same four texts were inscribed. On the outside of this case was the letter *shin*. The case was sewn to a similar base and had the same thong as the other. It was placed on the boy's forehead and the strap was knotted in the shape of the letter *daleth*. The ends hung forward over the shoulders. These three letters, *shin, daleth* and *yodh*, made up the consonants of the divine name *Shaddai*, the almighty.

Mary was skilled in the art of dyeing. As wool came from the sheep, she washed it with wood ashes and then dyed it before spinning. For this purpose she used murex shell from Tyre and indigo from India for the deep blue. For dyeing yellow she used almond leaves, and pomegranate bark supplied her with black, while green grapes pressed with water made a beautiful lush green. The new *talith* was woven of the finest wool with beautiful multi-colored stripes.

As Jesus wore now for the first time the phylacteries with the *tephillin*, the leather strips falling over the shoulders, wrapped into the big talith, the old familiar prayers took on a new meaning, and a strange, deep emotion stirred His soul. After evening prayer Joseph turned to Him and said, "Shalom, Jesus, son of David."

This was in the middle of the winter and Jesus would have to wait three months for the Feast of the Passover. How His heart longed for the house of God! The next time He came to Jerusalem He would be a "son of the Law," no longer subject to His parents.

This 12th birthday terminated His school years. Now whenever He had some free time in the evenings, for instance, when the sun came out for a little while in these rainy months, He would climb up the hill behind the town. There He would stand and look toward the south, toward Jerusalem with the house of the Lord. And he would again feel the great hunger of His soul to be again in His Father's house.

CHAPTER
9

THE SON OF THE LIVING GOD

There were three routes from Nazareth to Jerusalem. One might take the direct road due south across the rolling plain of Esdralon, then up into the hills of Samaria and over to the mountains of Judea. The distance is about 85 miles, a journey of four or five days on foot. This road was not always safe because the Samaritans were very bigoted and resented anyone's passing through their territory with faces set toward Jerusalem.

There was always a second caravan used around Passover time by those who wanted to avoid Samaria altogether by traveling to the eastern bank of Jordan, through the country of the Decapolis, and crossing into Judea near Jericho, but this way the length of the journey was almost doubled.

Then there was a third possibility: to go west to the seashore, pass by Mount Carmel and follow the old caravan route which leads from Damascus into Egypt. Near Lydda one would have to leave the highway and go on footpaths through the Judean Mountains to Jerusalem.

When Jesus was a young boy His parents used to take the shortest road through Samaria. Later, when Jesus could walk to school and His father no longer bothered with the donkey, they went alternately one year on the eastern banks of the Jordan and another year on the seashore so that they might view the beautiful country.

This year, when they asked Joseph whether he had any special choice, it is quite possible that he chose the shortest route, although he knew that traveling through Samaria might be quite disagreeable again. The little country between native Galilee and the mountainous Judea was inhabited by a strange people.

After the fall of the Northern Kingdom in 722 B.C., the Assyrians had taken most of the Jews away with them into captivity. In order to repopulate the country, they sent colonists over from Assur and settled them between Galilee and Judea. Gentiles by birth, they were soon no longer Gentiles in religion. They adopted the faith of the Israelites who had remained in the country, intermarrying with them. They took the five books of Moses for their sacred Scriptures. But they stopped. They were not willing to accept either the authority of the Prophets or the traditions so dear to the Pharisees. In Jerusalem they were regarded as dangerous heretics. While they worshiped the same God as the Jews, read the same Torah and regarded Moses as their supreme law-giver, they were nevertheless more hated than the Gentiles. The Samaritans, in turn, hated the Jews. Finally, they were solemnly excommunicated in the name of Jahweh.

They built a rival temple on Mount Gerizim and appointed their own high priest, who gathered around him priests and Levites. They married pagan women. The Jews broke off all relations, and the old traditional hatred was revived in all its bitterness. In Jesus' time the relations between His people and the Samaritans were worse than ever. To call a man "a Samaritan" was the gravest insult. A Jew would only say that when he had exhausted his vocabulary.

At the border before entering Samaria the leader of the pilgrimage would solemnly remind the pilgrims, "The Samaritan land is clean, the water is clean, the habitations are clean and the roads are clean," meaning that Samaria is a part of the Holy Land and it might be traversed without the risk of becoming liturgically unclean.

But this year nothing made any impression on Jesus, neither the happy commotion of the start of the pilgrimage, nor any of the many little incidents along the road. His mind was filled with but one thought: the temple. That was the place where His Heavenly Father dwelt. There alone one could offer sacrifice. The spotless lambs would be slaughtered again and burned at the entrance of the holy house.

With every step closer to the Holy City He felt the attraction toward the house of God as He had never felt it before. Here we touch on a great mystery in the life of Jesus, unfathomable to any human mind, known in the church always as hypostatic union.

Early in His earthly existence He began to say "Father" not to Joseph but to one within Him. Even while He was sitting at the feet of Joseph or His teacher in the synagogue, learning to read and memorizing the Law and the Prophets, He knew himself as being one with the Father.

While He was increasing "in wisdom, age and grace before God and man," He possessed all treasures of wisdom and knowledge through the huge court of the Gentiles. He comprehended its deep significance. This Court was a sign that all nations from the earth had been called to adore the one true God, the creator of heaven and earth. Then He came to the low wall where tablets warned in Latin and Greek: No Gentile may enter under penalty of death.

With holy awe He went through the barrier and hurried up
the steps which brought Him to the great altar of sacrifice.
It was streaming with blood. On the day before the *Pasch*
thousands of lambs were being slaughtered. There was nothing but blood. He knew all these sacrifices were a symbol
for the one sacrifice that was to come. He looked up toward
the entrance of the holy house with its mysterious curtain
behind which dwelt the living God, there in the temple forever; the Son was to be sacrificed and consumed instead of
all those lambs; to give His last drop of blood that the Father might take away the sins of the world.

The Father now accepted His offerings, but this time
He commanded only one thing: that when it was time to
leave again for Nazareth He must stay behind and spend
three days in the temple.

He could not do otherwise in order to to fulfill the
word which the Father had given Him. The hours which He
spent facing the house of gold, completely lost in contemplation, flew like so many moments.

Then the Father sent Him to the doctors. Within the
great temple enclosure, in one of the famous porticos, the
learned doctors of the Law lectured all day during the days
of the feast, and as long as crowds lingered behind. For
those living far from Jerusalem this was the only opportunity to hear famous men explaining the Law.

It was quite customary for the people to ask questions
of the experts of the Law, and these men loved to be con-
sulted. But the questions the Father bade Him ask were such
that only He and the Son knew the answer. There were in-
tricate points of the Law and complicated paschal questions. Then the most pressing problem of all was discussed:
the coming of the Messiah in the light of the Prophets.

At first the scribes were merely interested, but when
none of the leading rabbis of Israel could find an answer,

Jesus gave crystal-clear explanations, revealing a most profound understanding. They began to ask one another, "Who is this boy whose accent gives Him away as a Galilean? Where did He acquire His profound knowledge? Never before did anyone speak like this boy!" After the crowd was dismissed, they invited Him into their company. They wanted to hear more of the things of God.

After three days, His parents found Him in the temple sitting in the midst of the doctors. Day and night Joseph had been tortured by the thought that not only had they lost Him, but also that He had lost them and must have been trying to rejoin them. Mary knew He had not lost them. He had left them deliberately. She said to Him, "Son, why have you treated us so? Behold, your father and I have been looking for you anxiously" (Luke 2:48).

Never in all those 12 years had He given them any reason for grief. It hurt Him deeply when He had to answer in a way He knew would make them sad: "How is it that you sought me? Did you not know that I must be in my Father's house?" (Luke 2:49).

Poor Joseph! He who in all these years had been called "Father," now heard his son, in front of everybody, refer to God as His true Father.

Then His time was over. He rose, shalomed reverently before the venerable elders, as became one of His age, and went with His parents to Nazareth.

How quickly the gossip had traveled ahead and met them as they returned home. Inquisitive neighbors and cousins rushed to their door to besiege the poor parents with questions: "Where did you find Him? What did He do? How long did you search for Him? Is it true that He was sitting with the doctors? What did He mean when He said He must be about His Father's business?

The young man's stay in the temple was not only a

manifestation of himself to the doctors, but also a revelation to His mother and Joseph, and to all His relatives. Not all of them would take it in good faith.

It touched Him to the heart to see with what great humility Mary and Joseph waited for what He was going to do. Perhaps He must be about His father's business from now on and take up the career of a rabbi? They watched anxiously to see whether He would now put His things in order and take leave to spend His days with the scribes in the temple. According to the old saying, "Anyone who wants to assume riches should go to Galilee, but he who wants to strive for wisdom has to go to Judea."

When He simply resumed His daily duties as if nothing happened, helping His mother in the morning with the water and with the turning of the grindstone and, later on, spending His hours with Joseph in the workshop, their apprehension left them slowly.

How He admired Mary and Joseph in their complete submission to the will of God! The shock and the pain of the three days loss, the terrible searching, they remembered it all, not with resentment, but with joy. What a privilege to have been allowed a glimpse into the secret of the Divine Son and His Heavenly Father and to accept the suffering that such knowledge involved. The Father had taught them the great lesson: "He who loves father and mother more than me is not worthy of me" (Matt. 10:37).

CHAPTER
10

WHEN THE KING WAS CARPENTER

N ow it was the will of the Heavenly Father that Jesus
should devote most of His time to learning Joseph's
trade, that He should become a carpenter. "Love
labor and teach it to your sons," the Rabbi Shenaiah had
said.

As a small boy Jesus had learned by watching; now
He began to share the important decisions of a mature
craftsman. Father and son went together to select large logs
brought in by woodcutters from the wooded hills around
Nazareth. The choice was always difficult, and from Joseph,
Jesus learned to appreciate the beauty of sycamore, poplar,
terebinth, olive, chestnut, and oak trees. He must pick logs
which would be good for doors or window frames; He must
select slender rods to be made into handles. He learned,
too, that one of the worst crimes was to cut down a tree
which belonged to someone else. He also learned that to
call a man a *Qoses ben Quses*, a "cutter and a son of a cutter,"

was almost as bad as calling him a "Samaritan," and one must never buy from such a person.

Back at home, Joseph showed how to fasten the new log to the carpenter's bench, how to hew it roughly into shape with a hatchet, broad axe, and saw, or how to work it with a plane. Sometimes the vise, the plummet, and its cord were more important.

In this way Jesus learned also cabinetmaking, as the father carpenter showed Him how to create household furniture such as cedar chests, cupboards, window frames, doorframes, low tables and all kinds of farm implements.

Nazareth was a small country town surrounded by little farms, so there were frequent calls to repair tools around the neighboring slopes and hills. Together, father and son produced handles for pitchforks, threshing blades, hoes, wooden yokes for oxen, and wooden plows. He also learned to help in the construction of house frames, handling the large heavy beams, or making roofs with a layer of thorns and clay.

Much skill and strong labor were needed to work such rough timber into beams or plows. As the two carpenters worked side by side in the courtyard, their heads covered against the burning sun, the young man Jesus may have said lovingly to Joseph, "My Father in Heaven, the builder of the universe, has given me on earth a father who is a builder, also."

Joseph, stopping to lean on a half-worked plow, may have answered, "The first king in Israel was taken from behind the plow; another was called from the sheepfold; and the second David, the Messiah of Israel, will come from a carpenter's shop."

CHAPTER
11

THE POWER OF THE TONGUE

A group much berated in local talk were the priests at
Jerusalem. What embittered the people most was that
these authorities in Jerusalem did not conceal their
contempt for Galileans. Loftily they announced that no
Galilean was well versed in the Law, and that their Aramaic dialect was nothing short of ridiculous. Galileans were
simply comical "northerners."

About this, the "northerners" found much to say
among themselves. As long as Jesus was a small child, His
parents sent Him away whenever such talk occurred or
criticism of the chief priests began. Mary and Joseph felt
very keenly that even if priests did not live up to their high
office they were nevertheless the first servants of the Most
High. After Jesus' 12th birthday, however, He was allowed
to stay. In silence He listened to remarks on the accumulation
of wealth through shady transactions in the temple, on the
lack of faith of so many who were Sadducees and did not

believe in life after death, and especially on their treacherous compromising with the Roman authorities. Many elaborate tales were recounted with relish: the chief priests were taking what should have gone to another of lower rank; they were visiting the threshing floors to get a much larger amount of the harvest than what was due them; they had been beating the people with rods within the very temple grounds.

In the hot summer months most families would ascend to their flat rooftops to catch the cool evening breeze, and very animated conversations would go on from roof to roof. There was one topic in which all children were most interested: news of any recent caravan that had passed outside of Nazareth. From the hill behind the town, they could often see, after the rainy season, great caravans coming and going on the old route from Babylon into Egypt.

In Seluceia on the Tigris River there was a large Jewish population which had a flourishing trade with Alexandria, Egypt. Caravans of 50 camels and more passed by Nazareth from Damascus to Alexandria. The return trip always followed the coastal road for about 30 days, all the way to Antioch. From there they would cross the desert, taking about twice the time again to reach home.

These large caravans traveled on dirt roads baked by the sun and hardened by traffic. The bridges over streams and rivers were kept in repair by the Roman government and there were always hundreds of Roman soldiers along the way, the best protection against robbers.

Whenever such a large caravan was in sight, men from Nazareth would go to meet and trade with the camel drivers. In the evening, from rooftop to rooftop, they told of what they had heard and seen: of furs and hides from Persia, of embroideries and carpets, beautifully carved ivory work and pottery. There would be silks in all colors from China, and perfumes, rugs and pearls from India. Sometimes there were even tigers from India, which, together with lions from the jungle on the Jordan, would be sent to Rome for the games in the Coliseum.

On the return trip from Alexandria there would be papyrus, parchments, and beautifully copied scrolls of the Scriptures. Rich men in both Egypt and Babylon arranged regular caravans for which one could buy a ticket, and travelers, students or men with business in foreign parts, often took the opportunity.

The broker who handled the arrangements did not travel with them. He was usually a wealthy man in Alexandria or Antioch who managed several caravans. With the profits he would buy great vineyards and thousands of slaves, or hundreds of horses and camels which could then be rented to the travelers. Both the animals and the cargo of such a caravan were insured against loss, and these rich brokers had their own inns at certain intervals, always near a fort or a town where the caravans might pitch tents, or pitch camp at night.

Small children in Nazareth were curious and intrigued to learn that one merchant in the caravan had sets of false teeth to be sold in the bazaars in Jerusalem. At the next feast in the Holy City they searched eagerly around the marketplace until they found what they sought: animal or human teeth fastened together with gold bands and filled with cement!

But even talk about a caravan, however it might excite childish imaginations, would often end in petty complaints from those who envied the rich, and cursed their own fate which had put them into modest circumstances.

James and Jude were often with Him, as together they silently listened to such argument and discussion among the elders. Afterwards they would come to talk among themselves of how very difficult it is not to sin with the tongue.

James frequently quoted a favorite proverb: "Death and life are in the power of the tongue, and those who love it will eat its fruits" (Prov. 18:21).

A fitting end to such a discussion would be, "If any one makes no mistakes in what he says he is a perfect man" (James 3:2). Most conversations and most discussions would usually point to the most important subject — the coming of the Messiah.

CHAPTER
12

THE SHADOW OF THE CROSS

The Messiah was the hope of an invaded country longing for the end of Roman culture. One generation before Jesus was born Roman legions marched across Syria, taking the little kingdom of Judea by force and incorporating it into the mighty Roman Empire. At that time the Roman Empire comprised almost the whole of the then-known world. The many diverse races retained much of their own culture, customs, and religion, but Roman law, Roman governors, and Roman legions united them all.

As with other invaded countries, so it happened to little Palestine: first came the soldiers of the occupation army, then soon afterward their families with teachers who brought another culture and another religion into the country known as the "Holy Land of the Chosen People."

The Romans had only Greek teachers (usually slaves) for their children, the Greek language was predominantly spoken, and a Greco-Roman civilization spread rapidly over the little land. Pagan games and sports were introduced to the young people and pagan ideas and ideals were taught. The many Gentiles who lived in Galilee were easily won to such innovations and, worst of all, King Herod would not be outdone in servility. He wanted to have a good name with the Romans. He therefore built a marble temple to the Roman god Panias. He called his new capital "Caesarea." He rebuilt the city of Samaria, and gave it the name Sebaste, the Greek word Augustus. He favored the new religion and the new philosophy.

In Judea, teachers and rabbis were greatly worried. They tried to keep children away from the sports and games, and occupy them with even more strict religious training and religious services. But in spite of all their vigilance, the pagan influence was pushed more and more upon their young people.

The elders of the nation found their sole consolation, therefore, in the thought of the coming Messiah. All gloom would disappear from their faces as they talked in eager anticipation of the revolution the Messiah would bring about. More than any other generation, Jesus and His schoolmates were trained to find all references to the Messiah-King in the books of the Law and the Prophets.

The teaching about the Messiah is fundamental in the Old Testament. In the first book God said to the serpent, "I will put enmity between you and the woman, and between your seed and her seed; he shall bruise your head, and you shall bruise his heel" (Gen. 3:15).

In the same book are the special prophecies that through the descendants of Abraham, Isaac, and Jacob all people of the earth shall be blessed.

Yet occasionally the young students wondered, *Was not the Messiah to suffer for His people? What of the prophecies of Isaiah and Jeremiah?* Their teacher's firm assurance that the Messiah would be the King of kings, that He might have nothing personally to do with misery and suffering, did not entirely convince them all.

Children memorized the prophecy of Balaam, "A star shall come forth out of Jacob, and a scepter shall rise out of Israel; it shall crush the forehead of Moab, and break down all the sons of Sheth. . . . By Jacob shall dominion be exercised" (Num. 24:17–19).

The fifth book of Moses describes the Messiah as a prophet like unto himself (Moses): "And the LORD said to me, 'They have rightly said all that they have spoken. I will raise up for them a prophet like you from among their brethren; and I will put my words in his mouth, and he shall speak to them all that I command him" (Deut. 18:17–18).

If the messianic prophecies in these early books were still somewhat general, they became much more individual and more specific in the time of the kings, when the Messiah is described as the "Son of David, King and Victor" and He is shown obviously to be a person. Teachers had their classes recite from Psalm 2, which describes how the Messiah, although surrounded by enemies, conquers them all:

> Why do the nations conspire, and the peoples plot in vain? The kings of the earth set themselves, and the rulers take counsel together, against the LORD and his anointed, saying, "Let us burst their bonds asunder, and cast their cords from us." He who sits in the heavens laughs; the LORD has them in derision. Then he will speak to them in his wrath, and terrify them in his fury, saying, "I have set my king on Zion, my holy hill."
>
> I will tell of the decree of the LORD: He said to me, "You are my son, today I have begotten you. Ask of me, and I will make the nations

your heritage, and the ends of the earth your possession. You shall break them with a rod of iron, and dash them in pieces like a potter's vessel" (Ps. 2:1–9).

The young students had to learn Psalm 72:

Give the king thy justice, O God, and thy righteousness to the royal son!

May he judge thy people with righteousness, and thy poor with justice! Let the mountains bear prosperity for the people, and the hills, in righteousness! May he defend the cause of the poor of the people, give deliverance to the needy, and crush the oppressor! May he live while the sun endures, and as long as the moon, throughout all generations! May he be like rain that falls on the mown grass, like showers that water the earth! In his days may righteousness flourish, and peace abound, till the moon be no more! May he have dominion from sea to sea, and from the River to the ends of the earth! May his foes bow down before him, and his enemies lick the dust! May the kings of Tarshish and of the isles render him tribute, may the kings of Sheba and Seba bring gifts! May all kings fall down before him, all nations serve him! For he delivers the needy when he calls, the poor and him who has no helper. He has pity on the weak and the needy, and saves the lives of the needy. From oppression and violence he redeems their life; and precious is their blood in his sight. Long may he live, may gold of Sheba be given to him! May prayer be made for him continually, and blessings invoked for him all the day! May there be abundance of grain in the land; on the tops of the mountains may it wave; may its fruit be like Lebanon; and may men blossom forth from the cities like the grass of the field! May his name endure for ever, his fame continue as long as the sun! May men bless themselves by him, all nations call him blessed! (Ps. 72:1–17).

With great pride the teacher explained that the Messiah would be not only a prophet and a king, but a priest forever; and the children were required to learn Psalm 110:1–7:

The LORD says to my lord: "Sit at my right hand, till I make your enemies your footstool." The LORD sends forth from Zion your mighty scepter. Rule in the midst of your foes! Your people will offer themselves freely on the day you lead your host upon the holy mountains. From the womb of the morning like dew your youth will come to you. The LORD has sworn and will not change his mind, "You are a priest for ever after the order of Melchizedek."

The Lord is at your right hand; he will shatter kings on the day of his wrath. He will execute judgment among the nations, filling them with corpses; he will shatter chiefs over the wide earth. He will drink from the brook by the way; therefore he will lift up his head.

They learned where the Messiah would be born because thus it is written: "But you, O Bethlehem Ephrathah, who are little to be among the clans of Judah, from you shall come forth for me one who is to be ruler in Israel, whose origin is from of old, from ancient days" (Mic. 5:2).

They heard that He would come through a mother, not through a human father. The prophet Isaiah said, "Behold, a virgin shall conceive, and bear a son, and shall call his name Immanuel" (Isa. 7:14;KJV).

The great prophet Jeremiah said about the Messiah, "Behold, the days are coming, says the LORD, when I will raise up for David a righteous Branch, and he shall reign as king and deal wisely, and shall execute justice and righteousness in the land" (Jer. 23:5).

A little later, Isaiah prophesies of Cyrus as a figure of the Christ, the great deliverer of God's people:

> Thus says the LORD to his anointed, to Cyrus, whose right hand I have grasped, to subdue nations before him and ungird the loins of kings, to open doors before him that gates may not be closed: "I will go before you and level the mountains, I will break in pieces the doors of bronze and cut asunder the bars of iron, I will give you the treasures of darkness and the hoards in secret places, that you may know that it is I, the LORD, the God of Israel, who call you by your name. . . .
>
> Shower, O heavens, from above, and let the skies rain down righteousness; let the earth open, that salvation may sprout forth, and let it cause righteousness to spring up also; I the LORD have created it (Isa. 45:1–8).

The prophet Ezekiel adds a new consoling feature in describing the Messiah as a good shepherd: "And I will set up over them one shepherd, my servant David, and he shall feed them: he shall feed them and be their shepherd.

And I, the LORD, will be their God" (Ezek. 34:23–24).

Even the younger boys noticed that the passages their teacher chose to be memorized had always to do with the Messiah as a King in triumph and victory, and splendor and glory, as in Daniel 2:44: "The God of heaven will set up a kingdom which shall never be destroyed, nor shall its sovereignty be left to another people. It shall break in pieces all these kingdoms and bring them to an end, and it shall stand for ever."

Or from the prophet Haggai: "The latter splendor of this house shall be greater than the former, says the LORD of hosts; and in this place I will give prosperity, says the LORD of hosts" (Hag. 2:9).

After His 12th birthday, when Jesus was declared "Son before the Law," He stopped going to elementary school, and now the higher studies began. On Mondays, Thursdays, and on the Sabbath the young men would sit at the feet of the teacher, being instructed in the writings of the great rabbis.

The years passed. At 18 Jesus entered the marriageable age, and on His 20th birthday He reached maturity.

What He had learned about the Messiah, either in school or by listening to the older men, could be summed up in a few sentences. The Messiah-King would set up a world government with Judaism as the universal religion. He would punish the enemies in Gehenna but He would lead the land to great national prosperity. All the exiled Jews would be called home and there would be a great reunion; from then on there would be peace between men and beasts, and peace between men and men.

This materialistic kingdom of great prosperity and glory — which would be such a contrast to present slavery and oppression — was all the people expected of the Messiah to come. Impatiently they waited for the return of Elias, which would be the sign of the approach of the great change. The moon would turn into blood and the great voice of God would shake the foundations of the earth.

Through the hard labor of years, the family of Joseph had saved enough to buy all the "Sacred Books," scroll by scroll, and in the evenings or on the Sabbath afternoons, they would take turns reading aloud to each other.

Then, Mary and her Son saw Joseph begin to fail. Suddenly and quite rapidly, his physical strength ebbed, while during the Scripture readings, his features would take on a hue and a glow as though a fire were burning within him. Solemnly, the lines of the scrolls foretold that the Messiah, besides being a priest forever, would also be a man of sorrow. "He had no form or comeliness that we should look at him, and no beauty that we should desire him. He was despised and rejected by men; a man of sorrows, and acquainted with grief; and as one from whom men hide their faces he was despised, and we esteemed him not" (Isa. 53:2–3).

They turned again to the words of the Psalmist:

> My God, my God, why hast thou forsaken me? Why art thou so far from helping me, from the words of my groaning? O my God, I cry by day, but thou dost not answer; and by night, but find no rest. Yet thou art holy, enthroned on the praises of Israel. In thee our fathers trusted; they trusted, and thou didst deliver them. To thee they cried, and were saved; in thee they trusted, and were not disappointed. But I am a worm, and no man; scorned by men, and despised by the people. All who see me mock at me, they make mouths at me, they wag their heads; "He committed his cause to the LORD; let him deliver him, let him rescue him, for he delights in him!" Yet thou art

he who took me from the womb; thou didst keep me safe upon my mother's breasts. Upon thee was I cast from my birth, and since my mother bore me thou hast been my God.

Be not far from me, for trouble is near and there is none to help. Many bulls encompass me, strong bulls of Bashan surround me; they open wide their mouths at me, like a ravening and roaring lion. I am poured out like water, and all my bones are out of joint; my heart is like wax, it is melted within my breast; my strength is dried up like a potsherd, and my tongue cleaves to my jaws; thou dost lay me in the dust of death. Yea, dogs are round about me; a company of evildoers encircle me; they have pierced my hands and feet — I can count all my bones — they stare and gloat over me; they divide my garments among them, and for my raiment they cast lots (Ps. 22:1–18).

The sacred writings had revealed the true story of the Anointed One of God, the King of kings, the Prince of Peace. Yes, He would be a King, but His crown would not be one of gold, but one of suffering. Yes, He would reign from a throne — not bedecked with jewels, but made of wood shaped in the form of a cross. Yes, He would conquer the universe, but only after He had gone through the dark gate of death because His kingdom would not be of this world.

After such moments in their little home there was always a great silence. A flame *was* burning within Joseph, and his weakness became more apparent. With each new reading, the fire of love and compassion was kindled, consuming him as the holocaust on the great altar in the temple was consumed by sacrificial fire. No word was said, no question was asked; it was not necessary. But in the shadow of the wood-shaped cross, three hearts were burning with love — love for one another and love for the Eternal Father in heaven who had ordained it all, whose name be praised, whose Holy name be adored.

THE HIDDEN LIFE

When Joseph died, Mary and Jesus wept. She had lost her husband, her guardian, and her best friend who had loved her with such an utterly unselfish love.

Jesus had grown to admire and love this "just man" who had always been so faithful and unselfish, so devoted and loyal, so obedient to the will of the Father, and so loving to his family and friends. No one ever would be nearer and dearer. Now he was gone. His spirit, just like the one of the poor man, "was carried by the angels to Abraham's bosom" (Luke 16:22). There Joseph, the silent, the just, the humble, would meet the company of the just who had preceded him. There he would be greeted by the spirits of Adam and Eve, of Abraham, Isaac, and Jacob, of King David, his glorious ancestor, and by the spirits of the little children who had died because the cruel Herod had wanted to kill the Messiah. There, too, were the spirits of Zacharias and

Elizabeth, of Joachim his father-in-law and Anna his mother. Together they rejoiced that "the salvation was at hand" and peacefully they awaited their ascension into heaven.

After the burial, Mary and Jesus returned home and began their new life together. The young man took over His heritage: the house and the courtyard (this was considered a separate piece of property), and all the household utensils belonged now to Him. At the same time He assumed all the responsibilities as the head of a family and His mother's protector. As her grown-up Son, He had to support and represent His mother. With Joseph's death He had become "the master of the house." Mary's duties continued to be the same: grinding meal and baking bread, carrying water and gathering fuel, spinning and weaving, cooking and washing.

Jesus replaced Joseph in the workshop and became the carpenter of Nazareth in the everyday routine of living — *ora et labora* — prayer and work. "Truly, thou art a God who hidest thyself, O God of Israel" (Isa. 45:15), the prophet Isaiah had cried. The poor home in an obscure country town, the ordinary occupation as an artisan and the simple family life were chosen by the Heavenly Father that the Son might teach His brethren one important lesson: perfection consists in doing ordinary things extraordinarily well.

God wanted the Son's life on earth to be not that of a hermit on a rugged mountain, but life in a family circle in a little house, between many houses, on a street in a small town. A social life in daily contacts with human beings, daily business, daily greetings, daily dealings with customers.

The great story of those long silent years of the hidden life was the togetherness between mother and Son. To understand this one must go back to the very earliest days of creation when God had created man according to His own image and likeness as man and woman. When Adam and Eve, clothed with the light as with a mantle, lived before God as holy children with their father.

Jesus and His mother lived together in the same house, but no words were needed; their souls were always closely united. And so together they advanced in wisdom and grace before God and man. During all those years the mother saw her Son, who was also the Son of God, working busily in a carpenter shop. She watched Him saw and plane wood, receive orders and deliver the finished work, year after year. How much longer would that continue? In what way would the redemption of mankind from their sins be finally accomplished? How would the Messiah manifest himself to His people? And where was John, the son of her cousin Elizabeth? According to the word of his father Zacharias he was to be precursor. He was to prepare the people for the coming of the Messiah. And when would all that come to pass that old Simeon had prophesied to her?

There was no answer to her silent questions, but that did not disturb her. She contemplated all these things and she persevered in silence as the handmaid of the Lord.

It would have only been natural that out of a genuine anxiety she might have spoken, but she had learned not to ask questions. Now she knew that her Son had to be about His Father's business and this knowledge was sufficient. When the father wished it, He would make it clear that His hour had come. Until then she remained in peace and quiet repose.

"You will . . . bear a son," the angel Gabriel had said to her, "and you shall call his name Jesus. He will be great, and will be called the Son of the Most High; and the Lord God will give to him the throne of his father David, and he will reign over the house of Jacob for ever" (Luke 1:31–33). And here was her Son making plowshares and other farm tools.

"And you, child, will be called the prophet of the Most High," old Zacharias had addressed his newborn son, "for you will go on BEFORE THE LORD TO PREPARE HIS WAYS, to give knowledge of salvation to His people in the forgiveness of their sins" (Luke 1:76–77).

For a long time no one had word from John who had vanished in the desert. "Behold, this child is set for the fall and rising of many in Israel, and for a sign that is spoken against" (Luke 2:34).

Simeon had addressed Mary in the temple: "A sword will pierce through your own soul also, that thoughts out of many hearts may be revealed" (Luke 2:35). As Mary pondered on the fate of the Messiah, as she learned it from Holy Scriptures, this mysterious sword pierced her heart ever deeper and deeper. The hidden life of Jesus at Nazareth was full of hidden suffering, but it was also filled with that one great hidden joy: to do the will of the Father! For this Jesus came into the world, and this is what He had to preach, first, through 30 years of silent example.

Between His 20th and 30th years He went to Jerusalem for all the big feasts. Each time He became more keenly aware that the house of His Father, the holy temple, was being desecrated and made into a den of thieves. When He listened to the teachings of the rabbis in the Hall of Solomon, or in the cloisters of the royal porch, He perceived each time more keenly how shallow and hair-splitting their doctrine had become, how they misunderstood the great commandment of the Sabbath, how ridiculous were their thousands of petty rules, how completely they had forgotten that the Sabbath was for men, and not men for the Sabbath. He knew that one day He must act. He was ready, waiting for the Father to give the sign, but the Father remained silent. His hour had not yet come. In these years He learned how hard it is for the human heart to wait. "Not my will, but thine, be done" (Luke 22:42) became His constant prayer. And no one knew the hour but the Father.

CHAPTER
14

THE HOUR

Then the news was brought to Nazareth that a great prophet was preaching in the wilderness of Jordan, and his name was John. "Repent, for the kingdom of heaven is at hand" (Matt. 3:2), was his message.

Mary understood and renewed her surrender to the holy will of the Father. Mary must have expected it when Jesus asked her whether He might accompany her to her sister's house. He shouldered the chest with her belongings and they left the house where they had spent so many peaceful years. His mother did not even linger to throw a glance over the courtyard and house.

Jesus entrusted her into the care of her sister's family and then bade them farewell. No one asked Him where He was going.

The Spirit of the Heavenly Father led Him to join John the prophet and ask for His baptism. "Then Jesus came from Galilee to the Jordan to John, to be baptized by him. John would have prevented him, saying, 'I need to be baptized by you, and do you come to me?' But Jesus answered him, 'Let it be so now; for thus it is fitting for us to fulfil all righteousness' " (Matt. 3:13–15). And, as He stepped out of the waters of the river, the voice of the Father made itself heard to all generations of man: "This is my beloved Son, with whom I am well pleased" (Matt. 3:17).

The Spirit of God, descending upon Him in the shape of a dove, led Him from His hidden life into the desert of temptation, and from there into the world of men. He was to bring the words of the Father to men that they might come to believe and to know that He and the Father are one and that we who see Him also see the Father.

BIBLIOGRAPHY

Daniel-Rops, Henri. *Daily Life in the Time of Jesus.* New York: Hawthorne Books, 1962.

_____. *Jesus and His Times.* New York: E.P. Dutton & Co., Inc., 1956.

Goldin, Hyman E. *A Treasury of Jewish Holidays.* New York: Twayne Publishers, 1952.

Guardini, Romano. *The Lord.* Washington, DC: Regnery Publishing, Inc., 1987.

Heaton, E.W. Biblischer Altagzeit Des Alten Testaments, Claudius Verlag, Munchen.

Mauriac, Francois. *Life of Jesus.* New York: David McKay Co., 1951.

Meschler, Maurice. *The Life of Our Lord Jesus Christ.* St. Louis, MO: Herder, 1950.

Miller, Madeleine E. and J. Lane Miller. *Encyclopedia of Bible Life.* New York: Harper & Brothers, 1944.

O'Shea, Denis. *Mary and Joseph, Their Life and Times.* Milwaukee, WI: The Bruce Publishing Co., 1949.

_____. *The Holy Family.* Dublin: M.H. Gill & Son, Ltd., 1944.

Prat, Ferdinand. *Jesus Christ: His Life, His Teaching, and His Work.* Milwaukee, WI: Bruce Publishing Co., 1950.

Ricciotti, Guiseppe. *The Life of Christ.* Milwaukee, WI: The Bruce Publishing Co., 1947.

Sheed, F.J. *To Know Christ Jesus.* Westminster, MD: Christian Classics, Inc.

Temple, Fr. *Pattern Divine.* St. Louis, MO: B. Herder Book Co.

William, Franz Michel. *Das Leben Jesus Im Lande Und Volke Israel.* Heber & Co., G.M.B.H. Derlagsbuchhandlung.

EPILOGUE

On a clear day in 1987, Maria von Trapp passed from this life to join her beloved Captain, and her Lord.

The picturesque home she had nurtured in Vermont echoed with the sounds of Austria; seven years prior to her death, Maria suffered the trauma of watching the Trapp Family Lodge burn to the ground. Through the efforts of her family, the lodge was rebuilt in 1983 and remains a centerpiece of the family's heritage. It continues to be enjoyed by many visitors each year.

In 1998, *The Sound of Music* returned to Broadway, and it is also receiving tremendous acclaim in Europe.

Today, Maria von Trapp's son Johannes directs the activities of the lodge in Stowe, Vermont. The first American-born von Trapp, he and the rest of the family continue the family tradition with gusto.

The new Trapp Family Lodge.

Trapp Family Lodge
700 Trapp Hill Rd.
P.O. Box 1428
Stowe, VT 05672
1-800-826-7000 or (802) 253-8511